CONTENTS

PATRICK TAYLOR-MARTIN

JOHN
BETJEMAN

HIS LIFE AND WORK

ALLEN LANE

To my parents

ALLEN LANE
Penguin Books Ltd
536 King's Road
London SW10 0UH

First published 1983

Set in VIP Bembo
Filmset, printed and bound in Great Britain by
Hazell Watson & Viney Ltd, Aylesbury, Bucks

BRITISH LIBRARY CATALOGUING IN PUBLICATION DATA

Taylor-Martin, Patrick
John Betjeman.
  1. Betjeman, John—Criticism and interpretation
  I. Title
  821'.912   PR6003.E77

ISBN 0–7139–1539–0

PREFACE

This book does not set out to be the last word on John Betjeman. It will be some time before a definitive assessment of his achievement can be made. In a sense, of course, all judgements on writers are provisional; we never know what the next generation is going to make of them. Changing tastes may transport Betjeman into the stratosphere, displacing the reigning deities: Eliot, Pound, Joyce. (After all, in the field of architecture, Lutyens, once dismissed as a romantic reactionary, has returned to favour.) Then again, it may not.

Of course, it does not really matter who is 'in' or who is 'out'; or at least it should not matter. Academics with courses to run have to establish a manageable hierarchy in order to keep their examination papers to a reasonable length. The general reader should feel himself under no such constraint; he should be catholic in his tastes and prepared to trust his own judgement. Literature, let us not forget, exists to be enjoyed, not to be evaluated.

I enjoy Betjeman's poetry and I hope my book will help others to find similar enjoyment. My view of him is rather different, however, from that of some of his other admirers. Betjeman is a serious, not to say profound, writer rather than the facile light versifier some people take him to be. He does not endorse smug prejudices even if some of his readers are smugly prejudiced; he is aware (to use Henry James's words) of 'the black and merciless things which lie behind great possessions'. Readers who doubt this should look at him again.

★

A writer needs encouragement and praise as much as advice or practical criticism. Several friends have provided me with these during the writing of this book: I am grateful to them all. However, I should make particular mention of Philip Beason (who suggested the subject to me) and Lindsay Wolton (who helped type an almost indecipherable first draft). I owe a special debt to Mr John Guest of Allen Lane for the endless trouble he has taken on my behalf and for his continuous interest in the book from the time he first saw it in typescript. Without him, I do not think it would have been published.

Finally, I should like to thank Sir John Betjeman himself for having read the book in typescript at a time when he was far from well and also very busy with his own work.

P.T.-M.

All sources for quotations about Betjeman in the text are given in the Select Bibliography at the end of the book.

The author would like to thank John Murray Ltd for permission to quote extensively from Sir John Betjeman's published writings.

INTRODUCTION

Sir John Betjeman is a national institution. Awarded the C.B.E. in 1960, knighted in 1969, appointed Poet Laureate in 1972, he is, for most people, the one contemporary poet they have heard of and read.

The list of honours and public appointments is a long one: Companion of Literature, Fellow of the Royal Institute of British Architects, Queen's Gold Medallist, recipient of numerous literary prizes and honorary degrees. He was even, rather unexpectedly, Professor of Poetry at the University of Cincinnati in 1957. In addition, he has been a Royal Fine Art Commissioner and a Governor of the Anglican Study Group at Pusey House in Oxford. For some years now he has been indisputably a part of the literary Establishment.

As well as being a uniquely popular poet, he is a familiar broadcaster. Usually he is seen pottering about in old buildings or singing the praises of the railways before nationalization and standardization but he does not consider it beneath his dignity to appear on *Jim'll Fix It* in order to present a badge to a five-year-old poet. He is an active campaigner for the preservation of piers and other pieces of Victoriana which bureaucrats find inconvenient to maintain. It is his name which is most frequently appended to letters to *The Times* protesting against the imminent demolition of an unfashionable and unwanted building, be it the old Euston Station or a row of shops. The thriving Victorian Society owes much of its success to his imaginative advocacy of this once despised style. As has so often been said, with so much to do it is a wonder that he finds time to write poems at all.

When one thinks of Betjeman today, it seems hardly credible that
he was once the frivolous young undergraduate whom C. S. Lewis
considered to be no more than a 'pretentious playboy' and whose
poem on a City church was held up to ridicule by a sixth-form
master at Marlborough. Betjeman was unique and had to wait for
others to catch up with him, to learn to love the things he loved.
The interest in Victorian architecture which once seemed merely a
sophisticated pose has now acquired academic respectability. What
to begin with had the appearance of affectation has, in the end,
helped make him one of those national eccentrics on whom the
English dote. In England, *enfants terribles* have a way of turning into
Grand Old Men.

Nevertheless, in spite of his indisputable originality and uniqueness and the honours which have been conferred upon him,
Betjeman is still regarded with suspicion in some quarters. As Philip
Larkin observed in 1971, 'the quickest way to start a punch-up
between two British literary critics is to ask them what they think
of the poems of Sir John Betjeman'.

When the *Collected Poems* appeared in 1958, it made publishing
history by becoming an immediate best-seller. The first edition sold
something like 100,000 copies. Subsequent editions have brought
this total to over a million. For parallels, it is necessary to go back
to Byron and Tennyson. Certainly, no twentieth-century poet –
except, perhaps, Masefield – has achieved such popularity.

Academic critics naturally assumed that nothing which was
popular with the general poetry-hating public could be any good.
Had not Eliot declared, in his magisterial way, that 'poets in our
civilization, as it exists at present, must be difficult'? Betjeman, like
Hardy, Edward Thomas and Housman, was not 'difficult' in the
sense that Eliot meant. And, while he dealt with the major themes,
he compounded his sin by being entertaining as well. By writing
poems which were bought and read by the sort of people who did
not normally read poetry, it was almost as if he had done something
slightly discreditable, almost as if he had brought poetry into
disrepute. The idea that poetry could give pleasure, or that it might
be read without recourse to some scholarly gloss which told you
what it meant, went against the academic grain. Academic critics
resented the fact that philistines who had always hated modern
poetry because it was difficult and did not rhyme had found, at last,
a poet they could understand. Their hostility resolved itself into a

neat syllogism: the bourgeoisie was contemptible; Betjeman was loved by the bourgeoisie; therefore, Betjeman was contemptible. In fact, it was the syllogistic logic which was contemptible.

John Wain was typical of Betjeman's detractors. He disapproved strongly of those of Betjeman's social attitudes – regret for the passing of the Victorian world, distaste for the masses – which were shared by his smug middle-class, middle-brow readership. He dismissed the poet's craftsmanship as mere manipulation of hackneyed verse forms – 'most of his poems are written either in hymn-metres or in metres usually associated with "light" or comic verse' – and said that it required 'no more skill than is shown by the men who write the jingles on Christmas cards'.

Wain was not alone. The first edition of Anthony Thwaite's survey of *Contemporary English Poetry* (1959) as well as the *Scrutiny*-inspired *Pelican Guide to English Literature* (1961) ignored Betjeman completely. Betjeman's verse was considered light and undemanding, the jokes about it being 'non-U' to say 'toilet' and 'serviette' were seen as appealing to suburban social climbers by giving them the feeling that they were in the know. It all seemed to have less than nothing to do with poetry.

The hostility was as much social as literary. That Betjeman was known to be on good terms with members of the aristocracy and the royal family, that he was Princess Margaret's favourite poet, that he was a communicating member of the metropolitan literary smart set was not exactly counted in his favour. The late fifties and early sixties were the fag-end of the Angry Decade. There was a widespread contempt (particularly amongst the young) for that tight-knit world of top people to which Betjeman was known to belong. The prevailing literary fashion was for working-class social realism – Alan Sillitoe's *Saturday Night and Sunday Morning* had also appeared in 1958 – and there was a natural tendency to disparage the 'candelabra and wine' writers of the past.

Betjeman's habitual frivolity did not help matters either. He did not seem to want to be taken seriously as a poet and happily referred to himself as 'the Ella Wheeler Wilcox *de nos jours*'. He was photographed by Cecil Beaton dozing on a bench on the Embankment; wore a boater; dressed up in Henry James's morning clothes; and, worst of all, still harboured a childhood teddy bear called Archibald. It all deepened the suspicion that here was not a serious poet but rather a consummate showman who had been taken up by those dubious figures who ruled literary London, and who had all been at Oxford together, whose work appealed to the general public only because it made no demands on them.

But Betjeman is something more than a popular poet even if one does not despise popularity. He always had admirers outside the smart literary coteries and other than Book of the Month Club literati. Edmund Wilson ranked him with Auden and Dylan Thomas. Auden dedicated *The Age of Anxiety* to him and edited a selection of his poems and prose writings, *Slick But Not Streamlined*, which appeared in America in 1947. In his introduction he wrote, 'It is one of my constant regrets that I am too short-sighted, too much of a Thinking Type to attempt this sort of poetry, which requires a strongly visual imagination.'

Philip Larkin has made even larger claims for Betjeman, considering him to be a poet of equal if not greater importance than Eliot, and in his controversial *Oxford Book of Twentieth Century English Verse*, he gave Betjeman more space than Dylan Thomas. For Larkin, Betjeman's very popularity is invigorating. He upholds him as the poet who has reopened the channel of communication between the poet and the intelligent lay public, as 'the writer who knocked over the "No Road Through to Real Life" signs' which academic commentators had erected around contemporary poetry. Larkin regards 'the culture mongering activities of the Americans Eliot and Pound' and all that is implied by the term 'modernism' with the deepest suspicion. He distrusts the notion of 'difficulty' as an essential attribute of a successful work of literature and believes that the whole 'critical light industry' which has sprung up to explicate such works is part of a vast conspiracy. He admires Betjeman precisely because 'he is a poet for whom the modern poetic revolution has simply not taken place'. Betjeman, to Larkin's delight, turns his back on the wilful obscurity of much modern poetry and 'addresses himself to his art in the belief that poetry is an emotional business, that rhyme and metre are means of enhancing that emotion, just as in the days when poetry was deemed a kind of supernatural possession'. In other words, Betjeman achieves what Sir Leslie Stephen, in his essay on Gray, said was the ultimate aim of all poets, 'he touches our hearts by showing his own'.

Although Larkin is almost alone in considering Betjeman to be the equal of Eliot ('Can it be that, as Eliot dominated the first half of the twentieth century, the second half will derive from

Betjeman?'), critics generally are more inclined to allow him some merit, either as a talented outsider or as a respectable *petit maître*, than they were twenty years ago. Though hostility persists in some quarters, it would be surprising now to encounter a view as hostile as John Wain's or to find a book on modern poetry which ignored him completely. After all, a poet who has been admired by both Auden and Larkin cannot be dismissed as irrelevant for ever.

The shift in critical opinion is not just the result of a change in literary fashion. His 'snobbery' has come to be seen for what it is, a romantic yearning for variety and eccentricity rather than a narrow taste for the society of 'top people'. His 'conservatism', which is totally apolitical, is seen not as a facile endorsement of the status quo but as a plea for unplanned untidiness and diversity against the activities of bureaucrats and property speculators who think only of efficiency – a hateful word to Betjeman – and profit. He is no conventional 'little old man of the Right'. Although few share his nostalgia for the vanished aristocratic order, other views of his – particularly about what is now called the 'environment' – have gained wider currency over the years. Betjeman has, in fact, helped to create the taste which now enjoys him.

If Betjeman is a conservative it is because he genuinely wishes to conserve something which he thinks valuable: the sense of community and belonging rather than urban alienation; each town and city with its unique character rather than anonymous jungles of glass and concrete; a countryside with hedgerows rather than barbed wire dividing fields; pubs with natural beer rather than mass-produced keg. Betjeman is a reactionary in that he distrusts progress and believes that change is, more often than not, for the worse. He hates big business and the profit-motive with as much fervour as any Marxist. The property developers who destroy communities – he has even called it a kind of 'robbery' to deprive people of their familiar surroundings in this way – are the objects of his particular hatred.

These beliefs and values are part and parcel of Betjeman the poet. If there is really no such thing as 'pure' poetry, so there can be no such thing as 'pure' criticism. A writer's works spring from what he thinks, feels and believes. In Betjeman's case, this is particularly true. As Philip Larkin said many years ago, he is 'in the best sense a committed writer whose poems spring from what he really feels about life'. Nor are his beliefs shared only by the reactionary, the middle-aged, the middle-brow and the middle-class. In the sense that we support the aims of the Victorian Society, camp out on the roofs of scheduled buildings threatened by developers, join conservation groups, care about the environment, prefer the little streets of houses with their own gardens to the bleak high-risers, pay to ride in steam trains, drink real ale, buy fresh-baked bread, we are all reactionaries now.

CHAPTER ONE

POET'S PROGRESS

John Betjeman was born on 28 August 1906 in Highgate, the only child of Ernest Betjemann and his wife, Mabel Bessie Dawson. The Betjeman family had originally come from Holland in the late eighteenth century and set up as manufacturers of household articles for the rich in 1820. They originally spelt the name with one 'n' but in the 1860s added another because German-sounding names had become fashionable, particularly for manufacturers. Betjeman's mother dropped the second 'n' during the First World War, for obvious reasons. Betjeman appears in contemporary lists at Marlborough, however, as J. Betjemann, and his father always retained the 'German' spelling.

The family fortunes were founded on the Tantalus – a device for keeping the decanters out of the butler's pilfering hands – which was invented by the poet's grandfather and patented in 1821. This tradition of invention and craftsmanship was carried on by the family throughout the nineteenth century and the firm prospered. In *Summoned by Bells*, Betjeman lists some of the things they made:

> The Alexandra Palace patent lock,
> The Betjemann device for hansom cabs,
> Patents exhibited in '51,
> Improvements on them shown in '62,
> The Betjemann trolley used in coffee-rooms,
> The inlaid brass, the figured rosewood box,
> The yellow satinwood, the silverware –
> What wealth the money from them once had brought

To fill the hot-house half-way up the stairs
With red begonias; what servants' halls;
What terrace houses and what carriage-drives!

Although by the time Betjeman was born the family was less
prosperous than it had been, there was still his father's rambling
factory, an agglomeration of wooden sheds and workshops together
with brick-built offices and showrooms, in Pentonville Road,
Islington, as well as his uncle's factory in Birmingham, which made
glass, and a stoneworks in Torquay. Ernest Betjemann, the typical
Victorian paterfamilias, hoped that his son would carry on the
business, but he was to be disappointed.

In *Summoned by Bells*, Betjeman recalls the days when he and his
father would go down to 'the Works' by tram and how his father
would show him off proudly to the old workmen and travellers:
'Fourth generation – yes, this is the boy.' On these visits, he loved
to watch the craftsmen at work: black planks of mahogany coming
out smooth and sweet-scented under the plane in the cabinet-
makers' shop, the figured surfaces of rare woods emerging magically
as the French polishers, 'all whistling different tunes', swept their
cloths over them and, best of all, Buckland, in the silver-plating
shop, who would 'turn a penny into half-a-crown' to amuse him.
He would run from one workshop to another pretending to be a
train. If his father were still busy among his clerks in the counting-
house when he called on him at lunch-time, he would explore the
storerooms, some of them full of clocks or books, and, most
mysterious of all, a completely furnished drawing-room which he
discovered had been used by his great-grandfather when he lived
above the factory.

Interesting and exciting though these visits were, he could never
take any serious interest in the business. He could see no link
between the finished articles glowing in the showrooms or glistening
in Asprey's window and the fascinating things he saw the workmen
doing in the factory. His father, who designed many of the objects
himself, believed that he was 'creating beauty' but for his son there
was no beauty in these expensive artefacts, however skilfully made.
It was the beauty of the natural world which moved him rather than
the imagined 'beauty' of silver cigarette-boxes and leather dressing-
cases.

He failed at all the things his father wanted him to be good at. He

would clumsily drive the chisel into his hand when being taught
how to carpenter and when, anxious to pose as a country gentleman
in his tweeds, his father took him shooting or fishing, he would
make a fool of himself by forgetting to release the safety catch of his
gun or by talking too much and disturbing the fish. But Ernest
Betjemann was a kind and affectionate man and, in the early days at
least, his son loved him. He enjoyed, particularly, the long country
walks they took together, for his father loved the countryside and
delighted him with his knowledge of birds and flowers and trees.
He was also an amateur painter and liked to paint the landscape of
East Anglia and Cornwall, where the family took their holidays, in
the style of his favourite artists Constable and the Cornishmen,
Arnesby-Brown and Stanhope Forbes. He collected Georgian silver
and furniture and the two of them would visit antique shops, the
small boy watching, fascinated, as his father – who was almost
stone deaf – raised his deaf appliance to catch what the shopman was
saying.

In *Summoned by Bells*, Betjeman tells us:

> I knew as soon as I could read and write
> That I must be a poet.

It was this conviction, he believes, which made him so unsatisfactory
a son.

> I was a poet. That was why I failed.
> My faith in this chimera brought an end
> To all my father's hopes.

He still feels guilty about disappointing his father and forcing the
workmen to find other jobs when the business had to be sold. He
still flinches when he sees, in the bedroom of a country house in
which he is staying, an onyx ashtray or a dressing-chest that 'has
got a look about it of the Works'. The granite obelisk over the
family grave in Highgate Cemetery, he says, still seems to point 'an
accusing finger to the sky'.

It must have been particularly painful to discover that Evelyn
Waugh noted in his diary in December 1960: 'Betjeman's biography.
John demonstrates how much more difficult it is to write blank
verse than jingles and raises the question: *why* did he not go into his
father's workshop? It would be far more honourable and useful to

make expensive ashtrays than to appear on television and just as lucrative.'

Betjeman's early childhood in Highgate was happy. He loved the peace and security of the small house at 31 West Hill overlooking the Burdett-Coutts estate. Close by was Hampstead Heath with its grazing sheep and beyond spread the lost county of Middlesex. London began at the foot of their hill; it had not yet engulfed the entire region. Middlesex could still be called 'rural'. Perivale was 'a parish of enormous hayfields', and, from Greenford, instead of petrol fumes, 'scent of mayfields most enticingly was blown'. In those days, Evelyn Waugh's father could build a house in Golders Green which his son claimed was almost in the country.

The boon companion of these early years was, of course, his famous teddy bear, Archibald, who is still with him:

> Safe were those evenings of the pre-war world
> When firelight shone on green linoleum;
> I heard the church bells hollowing out the sky,
> Deep beyond deep, like never-ending stars,
> And turned to Archibald, my safe old bear,
> Whose woollen eyes looked sad or glad at me,
> Whose ample forehead I could wet with tears,
> Whose half-moon ears received my confidence,
> Who made me laugh, who never let me down.
> I used to wait for hours to see him move,
> Convinced that he could breathe. One dreadful day
> They hid him from me as a punishment:
> Sometimes the desolation of that loss
> Comes back to me and I must go upstairs
> To see him in the sawdust, so to speak,
> Safe and returned to his idolator.

A child's – particularly an only child's – devotion to a teddy bear is not uncommon. It is more unusual for the feeling to persist into old age. Betjeman's friends maintain that his affection for the battered old bear is genuine. He says he would even take Archie abroad with him but is frightened that over-zealous customs officials might rip him open searching for drugs. So, to make up for the separation, he writes him affectionate letters which his secretary has to read out. He wrote a strange little story about him for his own children during the thirties, which was eventually published as *Archie and the Strict Baptists* in 1977.

Betjeman believes that this unusually prolonged childhood fixation is a case of arrested development. If so, it seems a rather self-conscious one, irritating even. While in some ways the least affected of men, Betjeman has always fostered an image of himself as weak and vulnerable. There is a strong masochistic streak in those love poems in which he pictures himself as the puny lover of some Amazonian-thighed sports girl. In real life, even as a young man, he seemed to shuffle into rooms, giving the impression of being completely helpless and at sea though he invariably managed to get exactly what he wanted. It certainly struck jealous rivals as a cunning pose, a means of getting attention and sympathy. Betjeman has said that a psychologist once called him 'a dear child of twelve and a half'. He has found that with women as well as waiters, it is no bad thing to play this up. A case of arrested development or not, Betjeman has found the role of 'little boy lost' a very satisfactory one. Everyone plays a part but very few play it with complete success or are clever enough to choose the part which suits them best. Betjeman, with his shuffling walk, his helpless and defeated look, his crumpled collars, his teddy bear, his childish delight in all sorts of things ('Gosh, how lovely!'), is acting a part which suits him down to the ground. 'Take care of me,' he seems to say; and people do.

The need to be taken care of suggests a deeply wounded nature, a basic insecurity. His early sense of security in Highgate was shattered by a sadistic young nurse his parents took on to look after him. She used to lock him in dark cupboards, put him over her knee and smack him – 'fear confused with thrill' – and threaten him with humiliations such as being fed from a bottle or put back into nappies. His parents eventually dismissed her but not before much damage had been done. In those pre-Freudian days, parents were blissfully unaware of the effect which disturbing experiences of this kind might have on a sensitive child. Even very fond parents like Betjeman's quite willingly put their children in the care of women about whom they knew very little. Most of these women were kind and affectionate. Betjeman was unlucky – or lucky, of course, as these early experiences helped turn him into a poet. It was from this nursemaid that he first heard about hell at the age of five. She was convinced that she was going there and her passionate conviction infected the child with her own oppressive guilt and sense of sin,

her certainty of eternal damnation. It inspired one of his best poems,
'N.W.5 & N.6'.

Childhood also contained humiliations and fears of a more
tangible sort. He was, from the beginning, acutely conscious of the
rigid social hierarchy which governed the part of London in which
they lived. He knew his parents were 'a lower, lesser world' than the
carriage folk but were, at the same time, better off than their next-
door neighbours because they had a brougham and could afford to
take holidays by the sea. His first love, Peggy Purey-Cust, a pretty,
blonde, freckled little girl with blue eyes – 'all my loves since
then /Have had a look of Peggy Purey-Cust' – belonged to that
higher world which looked down on West Hill. The huge house
with its grand entrance hall, sweeping staircases and vast drawing-
room seemed a palace after his parents' modest villa. Her family
rather disapproved of him and when she was ill and he took her his
favourite book (a fairy story called *House of the Sleeping Winds* with
coloured illustrations in the style of Walter Crane) the gift was
received coldly by a servant. After several weeks, it was quietly
returned; Peggy Purey-Cust was 'gone for ever'. The sense of loss
has remained sharply with him.

In *Summoned by Bells* he recalls, too, an occasion in Cornwall
when a Miss Usher came down to organize the children's games.
She played with them all and was nice to them all, but 'somehow,
somehow', it seemed to the young Betjeman, 'not so nice to me'.

> What was it I had done? Made too much noise?
> Increased Miss Tunstall's headache? Disobeyed?
> After Miss Usher had gone home to Frant,
> Miss Tunstall took me quietly to the hedge:
>   'Now shall I tell you what Miss Usher said
> About you, John?' 'Oh please, Miss Tunstall, do!'
>   'She said you were a common little boy.'

The memory of the awful discovery that someone whose affection
he desperately wanted disapproved of him has remained. In fact, the
incident bit so deep into his consciousness that he has recounted it,
in rather different form, in more than one poem. He says he still has
feelings of inferiority and unworthiness and cannot understand why
people like him. They make his craving for affection and love all the
more intense, all the more poignant. He is still easily hurt and in
constant need of reassurance. Archibald, of course, can neither hurt

nor be hurt. Betjeman's dependence on him is not so surprising after all, perhaps.

Schooldays brought fear as well as humiliation and guilt. At his first school, Byron House, where he met Miss Purey-Cust, he was comparatively happy. But the harbinger of future woe came when two of his boyish rivals, one of whom he had previously thought a friend, ambushed him. These bullies followed him to Highgate Junior School where he arrived, red-capped and red-blazered, in 1914. Here the bullying increased and finding safe routes to walk home by became a conscious art. Now that the war against the Kaiser had started, his two old enemies took to taunting him because of his German-sounding name. They would dance around him, shouting:

> Betjeman's a German spy –
> Shoot him down and let him die:
> Betjeman's a German spy,
> A German spy, a German spy.

Such treatment deepened his sense of being an outsider: persecuted, vulnerable and set apart from his contemporaries.

He nevertheless had a refuge into which he could slip: his imagination. It was at Highgate that his love of poetry began to flower. He had been writing poems since about the age of six and his father encouraged him, giving the sound advice: 'Let what you write /Be funny, John, and be original.' He also presented him with a leather-bound manuscript book, stamped with his initials, into which he could copy his verses. One day at the Tate he had shown him Frank Bromley's narrative painting of *The Hopeless Dawn* in which a young wife and her mother-in-law look out anxiously from their cottage window at a storm-tossed sea as the candle gutters and the lost sailor's meal lies uneaten on the table. The painting is typical of Victorian sentimentality at its most mawkish but his father challenged him to translate it into verse and gave him his opening lines.

> 'Through the humble cottage window
>   Streams the early dawn.'
> The lines my father gave me sounded well;
> But how continue them? How make a rhyme?
>   'O'er the tossing bay of Findow
>   In the mournful morn.'

> With rising hopes, I sought a gazetteer –
> Findochty, Findon, Finglas, Finistère –
> Alas! no Findow . . . and the poem died.

Although Betjeman's early poems are of no importance in themselves, they are interesting in being attempts to write the same kind of poems which he has written in his maturity. This is something which could be said of no other modern poet. Eliot cannot have been groping towards *The Waste Land* at seven. But in Betjeman's case one is immediately aware that the poems he has written as a mature poet – or some of them, at least – would have appealed to him as a boy and seemed to him the kind of poems he was trying to write himself. It is another sign of the distance which separates him from almost all his contemporaries.

Betjeman is still fond of the poets – Hemans, Campbell, Long-fellow, Scott – who appealed to him as a boy. Like all children, he was chiefly attracted by rhyme. Unlike most contemporary poets, however, he has continued to regard poetry as a musical and sensuous art rather than as a vehicle for tortuous cerebration.

> My goodness me! It seemed perfection then –
> The brilliance of the rhymes AB, AB!

The impulse has remained the same even though the technique has improved. As Auden once observed, no young person who wants to write because he thinks he has things to say will ever succeed, but a young person who is attracted to writing because he enjoys 'messing about with words' might just be a poet. In a poem which he wrote at the age of thirteen when he was at the Dragon School and which was published in the *Draconian*, Betjeman is to be seen doing just that.

> Whatever will rhyme with Summer?
> There only is 'plumber' and 'drummer':
> Why! the cleverest bard
> Would find it quite hard
> To connect with the Summer – a plumber!

Auden might have added that no mature poet who loses touch with the fact that a poem must have a primal auditory attraction will be a good poet.

Betjeman has not only retained his early pleasure in metre but the inspirational source of his poems has remained the same too. His poems sprang then, as they do now, from his desire to preserve an incident, a scene, a place from the encroachments of time.

> My urge was to encase in rhythm and rhyme
> The things I saw and felt (I could not *think*).

His poetic imagination has remained resolutely visual. The only problem in those days was the gap between his 'feelings' and his 'skill'. Too often, he thought, the poems 'Came out like parodies of *A & M*' and it is interesting that this should be the gibe most often made today by people (John Wain, for instance) who dislike his work.

By a strange coincidence, there was on the staff of Highgate Junior School a young American master named Eliot, who was thought to be interested in poetry. In Betjeman's words,

> That dear good man, with Prufrock in his head
> And Sweeney waiting to be agonized . . .

Betjeman, immensely proud of his childish verses ('as good as Campbell now') decided to bind them into a book, *The Best of Betjeman*, and present them to Mr Eliot. As Philip Larkin has said, it is a scene 'worthy of a nineteenth-century narrative painter: "The Infant Betjeman Offers His Verses To The Young Eliot" '. Eliot, unfortunately, did not say whether he liked them or not; though 'A boy called Jelly said "He thinks they're bad".' What is more, it appears that Eliot never referred to this memorable occasion during any of their subsequent meetings.

Betjeman's childhood was not, however, composed solely of intimations of guilt, fear, anxiety and doubt, together with much humiliation in the form of bullying, and release of a provisional sort in the writing of poetry. He had an essentially normal childhood. His parents loved him deeply, with that kind of possessive affection of which the parents of an only child are alone capable. The knowledge that he was loved and valued by his parents must have counterbalanced the threats to his security which came from elsewhere. School was hateful, as it is to most sensitive and imaginative children, because of its insistence on conformity and its tendency to punish any deviation from the norm. Children, rather more than adults, are inclined to identify and persecute an outsider. With children he met away from school, Betjeman seems to have got on well. His poems about holidays in Cornwall are full of the names of other children – Joc, Audrey, Biddy, Joan – and clearly this companionship meant a lot to him.

His parents owned a house and some land at Trebetherick, a small village in north Cornwall. It was a rough and windswept part of the coast, with the huge Atlantic rollers breaking on Pentire further up the estuary and the treacherous sandbank, Doom Bar, regularly claiming its toll among the little fishing vessels which put out from Padstow. Betjeman has recalled how remote Cornwall was in those days. The natives were primitive children of nature, many of whom had never set foot outside the county and who regarded outsiders as 'foreigners'. The family would travel down on the London and South Western – the distance seemed immense – from Waterloo to Wadebridge and from there take the horse-brake for the remaining seven miles to Trebetherick. Their journey was over steep, un-metalled roads, very different from the prim, gaslit streets of Edwardian north London which they had left behind. Oil lamps or candles rather than bright electroliers flickered in the windows of the cottages. In fact, there were several villas which were owned by prosperous families such as Betjeman's, attracted by the remoteness of the place as well as the opportunity it afforded for healthy recreation – sea fishing and golf on the links at St Enodoc – and breathtaking views to tempt the amateur artist.

It was the sea and the coastline which fascinated Betjeman. The steep slate cliffs with tamarisk and sea-pink growing on them seemed as formidable as the Himalayas. The rock pools on the beach contained shrimps and starfish, a mysterious and brightly coloured underwater world. Games were played on the sand, dams built and destroyed. He learned to swim in the sea at Trebetherick: 'clean, medicinal and cold'. The countryside surrounding the village was hilly and remote, threaded by narrow lanes, banked high with wild flowers: foxglove, valerian, bugloss. He did not come to explore this rich hinterland with its granite hilltop churches – Blisland, St Minver, St Ervan, St Endellion – until he was somewhat older, however. The dark, cool depths of Shilla Woods seemed to contain a lurking terror and expeditions to nearby farms to collect the milk were fraught with danger from hissing geese and vicious farmyard dogs. Padstow, where they went shopping, crossing the estuary by ferry and eagerly watching for wrecks on Doom Bar, was tame and domestic by comparison, with its stationers' and fancy-goods shops full of knick-knacks to delight a child's eye; though even here there was the excitement of the quay frequented by the rough-looking fishermen who made their living from the town.

The effect which Cornwall and the sea, in all its moods, had on Betjeman's imagination is evident in his writing. He has returned to it time and again in poem after poem, particularly in his later ones. He has, in fact, continued to keep a house in Trebetherick, though his mother sold much of the land she owned when her husband died and she feared financial ruin. His granddaughter was named Endellion after the Cornish saint, whose church he knows and loves so well. His deep love of the county is seen as much in his prose writings – the brilliant essays on Padstow and on Blisland church from *First and Last Loves* as well as the early Shell Guide to the county which he compiled – as in his poems. Cornwall, as much as north London, was the place where he had his roots. It was, moreover, the place in which he had been happiest.

Schooling, nevertheless, had to run its inevitable course. After his few years at Highgate Junior School, it was decided to move him to the Dragon School (also known as Lynam's, after one of its headmasters) in Oxford. It was his first acquaintance with the place which he was to come to love almost as well as Cornwall. He was happier at this school than at any of his previous ones and made several friends, including the young Hugh Gaitskell whose parents rather disapproved of Betjeman because his family was in trade. He began to acquire the kind of deceitfulness a boy needs to protect him from his fellows, with the result that life was easier than it had been before. He even received a jolly encomium from his housemaster, Gerald Haynes, for the manly way he took a beating.

The Dragon School was more free and easy than most preparatory schools of the time and Christopher Hollis, who was at nearby Summerfields, recalls how he envied the young Draconians who were allowed to roam about in open-necked shirts. Betjeman owes much to the school and he acknowledges a special debt to Gerald Haynes, the huge, bespectacled master with a cigarette permanently stuck to his lower lip, who took the boys on expeditions into the country. Betjeman dedicated his collection of broadcasts and essays, *First and Last Loves*, which was published in 1952, to Haynes's memory and recalled him as the man 'who first opened my eyes to architecture'.

At the age of twelve Betjeman had the sort of passion for Gothic architecture which boys more usually lavish on model aeroplanes or motorcars.

> Can words express the unexampled thrill
> I first enjoyed in Norm., E.E., and Dec.? . . .
>
> *
>
> . . . Who knew what undiscovered glories hung
> Waiting in locked-up churches – vaulting shafts,
> Pillar-piscinas, floreated caps.,
> Squints, squinches, low side windows, quoins and groins –
> Till I had roused the Vicar, found the key,
> And made a quick inspection of the church?

He used to go cycling with Haynes, in search of churches and wild flowers, deep into the Oxfordshire and Northamptonshire countryside. He would continue his feverish pursuit of Gothic among the colleges and churches of the city, alone or in the company of a friend, for, rather surprisingly perhaps, Betjeman had friends who shared his unusual interests. At home in London – his parents had by now moved to a house in Church Street, Chelsea – he and his schoolfriend, Ronald Hughes Wright, would spend all day travelling on the underground so that they could soon boast an unexampled knowledge of the stations bounded by Finsbury Park to the north, Clapham Common to the south, Barking to the east and Acton and Ealing, with enticing metro-land and all of 'beechy Bucks' stretching beyond it to the west. Betjeman was already becoming a connoisseur of places, not just a lover of old buildings. This early interest in topography and architecture was a source of pleasure, an opportunity to escape from the dull confines of home and parents and see new places, rather than some precocious academic pursuit. His excursions were fun rather than attempts to fill notebooks and win prizes. He was, from the first, an amateur in the truest sense rather than a scholar.

At home in London he also began to frequent the second-hand bookshops in the Essex Road, from which he would come away loaded down with books like *Church Bells of Nottingham* and *Baptismal Fonts* as well as volumes of descriptive verses by those forgotten parson poets of the nineteenth century of whom his own poems contain so many echoes. Best of all, he liked volumes of steel engravings depicting views of London and Edinburgh and

Liverpool in the early nineteenth century: they fed his love of the past and fired his topographical imagination. Such books, now so valuable, could then be picked up for shillings. In Farringdon Road once, he even found an inscribed copy of Edward Lear's *Views in the Seven Ionian Islands*, which he bought for a shilling. The hope of other such discoveries lured him on.

Just as in his youthful poems Betjeman bore a marked resemblance to the poet he was to become, so in his precocious interest in architecture and suburban railways, the child was consubstantial with the man. Betjeman's tastes and interests set fair at a very early age. Not for him the years spent pursuing some interest that would eventually be cast aside. Betjeman has not just retained something of the child's freshness of vision; he has applied it to things which interested him then as much as they do now.

The move to Chelsea marked an increased prosperity. His vaguely arty mother enjoyed the thrill of living in a neighbourhood which still had a nineties air of decadence about it.

> For we were Chelsea now and we had friends
> Whose friends had friends who knew Augustus John:
> We liked bold colour schemes – orange and black –
> And clever daring plays about divorce
> At the St Martin's. Oh, our lives were changed!
> Ladies with pearls and hyphenated names
> Supplanted simpler aunts from Muswell Hill:
> A brand-new car and brand-new chauffeur came
> To carry off my father to the Works.

But Betjeman missed his beloved Highgate. The growing estrangement from his father made escape from the 'poky, dark and cramped' house a joy indeed. As well as the expeditions to bookshops in the Essex Road and the marathon train journeys, he took to churchgoing. On Sunday nights he would walk the deserted city in search of some out-of-the-way church, drawn on by the sound of its bell. He preferred the sort where a single parishioner sat before an absentee incumbent who had reluctantly dragged himself up from the country to perform the statutory offices which earned him his stipend. This precocious taste for the backwaters of the Church of England nourished both his love of human eccentricity and of the delicious past he had glimpsed in his books of engravings. He thinks also that these solitary expeditions to obscure churches helped allay the increasing sense of guilt which overspread the years of adolescence.

At thirteen Betjeman had been sent to Marlborough, an expensive and spartan public school in Wiltshire; the five years he spent there were the unhappiest of his life. At Marlborough, the casual bullying which he had experienced at his private schools assumed horrific proportions for it was, to a large extent, institutionalized, the older boys being given *carte blanche* to terrorize their juniors by the complacent beaks with their belief in: 'By the boys, *for* the boys. The boys know best.' In Upper School, authority was vested in a group of older boys, remarkable only for their athletic prowess, known as Big Fire. They were able to beat on the slightest pretext, but the most frightful torture they could inflict was to have their victim put in the basket. This ritualistic punishment was humiliating rather than painful and involved the offender being stripped to his shirt and forced into a huge wicker basket full of apple cores and waste paper as the other boys, Betjeman among them, gathered round, feeling 'goody-goody-good /Nice wholesome boys who never sinned at all'. Ink and treacle were then poured over the culprit's head and the basket hoisted up to the beams. Betjeman recalls the sight of the boy's eyes, like a frightened animal's, looking out between the slats of the basket as it swung high above them. Afterwards,

> They let the basket down
> And Angus struggled out. 'Left! Right! Left! Right!'
> We stamped and called as, stained and pale, he strode
> Down the long alley-way between the desks,
> Holding his trousers, coat and pointed shoes.
> 'You're for it next,' said H. J. Anderson.
> 'I'm not.' 'You are. I've heard.' So all that term
> And three terms afterwards I crept about,
> Avoiding public gaze. I kept my books
> Down in the basement where the boot-hole was
> And by its fishtail gas-jet nursed my fear.

Though Betjeman managed to avoid this major catastrophe, as he progressed through the school he showed no particular talent for anything either scholarly or athletic. He acquired a reputation as something of an eccentric and, on that account, perhaps, was tolerated. Louis MacNeice, who was a contemporary at Marlborough, remembered him 'with a face the colour of peasoup . . . a brilliant mimic but also a mine of useless information and a triumphant misfit'. He read voraciously and by the time he reached the sixth form his literary tastes had broadened out to include Aldous Huxley and the *London Mercury* though he remained loyal to his obscure nineteenth-century poets and books of views.

As Wiltshire was not particularly rich in church architecture, he forsook Gothic for the charms of the eighteenth century. He began to collect eighteenth-century books and read most of the poems in Dodsley's *Miscellany*, though, he says, 'without fully understanding them'. He admired the eighteenth century for its lightness and elegance, its artificiality of style. He even enjoyed surrogates like Austin Dobson's precious piece of nonsense, the *Ballad of Beau Brocade*. He continued to make sight-seeing expeditions and, near Marlborough, he discovered the disused grotto of Lady Hertford's mansion which had been turned into a potato store: through the iron grille, he was able to pick out the shell-work mouldering among the tubers. He also used to roam about in the spacious park of the seventeenth-century mansion at Ramsbury, longing to get inside and see its furniture and library, and has said that 'the mystery of its winding drive gave me a respect for the system of hereditary landowning which I have never shaken off'.

One of the few sympathetic masters at Marlborough was Christopher Hughes, a retired colonel, who used to take groups of boys on sketching expeditions in the Wiltshire countryside. 'We would sit in front of a thatched barn, a haystack or a row of summer elms and make a rough outline in pencil of what we saw, before applying the watercolour . . . All this industry was accompanied by talk about anything except sex. Then there was tea in a cottage with Wiltshire lardy cakes.' Though he was never much of an artist, he thinks these excursions taught him 'to appreciate the importance of the setting of a building, the shape of trees and the effects of light in different weathers and at different times of day'. All of which were valuable lessons for a poet whose imagination is primarily visual. Though no scholar or carrier-off of scholarships and prizes, Betjeman was fortunate throughout his school career in having teachers – Eliot, Haynes and Hughes – who were able to stimulate his imagination.

But, much as Betjeman liked Hughes, he soon began to disagree with him about art. Betjeman's eyes were opened to the neglected masterpieces of the nineteenth century by the steel engravings in the books he bought. Later, he read that pioneering work of architectural history, A. E. Richardson's *Monumental Classic Architecture in Great Britain and Ireland*, which had appeared in 1914. This book treated seriously, for the first time, those neglected and despised buildings of the Classical Revival such as St George's Hall in Liverpool and the British Museum in London. It was what Betjeman had been waiting for. Colonel Hughes considered such buildings ridiculous; in him antiquarian prejudice reigned undisturbed.

Betjeman discovered that Hughes was rather looked down on by the real aesthetes of the school led by two future art historians, Ellis Waterhouse and Anthony Blunt, both of whom became Betjeman's friends. It was from Blunt that Betjeman first heard about the Impressionists, the Italian primitives and the writings of Clive Bell and Roger Fry. He began to think the English school of landscape painters, admired by Hughes and his father, hopelessly provincial. He was soon maintaining that 'the Italians and the French are the only good painters', and taking an interest in Blunt's sophisticated school magazine, *The Heretick*, intended as a counterblast to the stuffy and orthodox *Marlburian*. Blunt had also formed an Arts Society which Betjeman joined and to which he read a paper, 'ridiculing, while half admiring, Victorian poets and artists' though he still thought their architecture 'was not to be taken seriously, as it was purely imitative and rather vulgar'.

With Betjeman's emergence as an embryonic aesthete went an increased langour. In a group photograph of about this period, he is to be seen in the middle row with his index finger delicately resting on his cheek in contrast with the folded arms of the stalwart youths who surround him. Such epicene sensitivity was an essential part of the aesthete's make-up; he must be as witty as Wilde and as dandified as Firbank. Betjeman recalls that at Oxford he identified himself with a hyper-sensitive plant in the botanical gardens which recoiled when someone's hand was held near it.

His father hated these signs of laziness, affectation and snobbery, seeing them as inimical to his determination that his son should carry on the family business. He was an irascible, impatient and intolerant man, easily moved to anger if things were not to his taste: if his bacon happened to be cold, the whisky undecanted or the potatoes at dinner too hard. Betjeman's devout Christian Scientist mother – anxious and ill and self-pitying – did her best to appease him and to mediate between father and son. Their rows were an agony to her, though one she was not above melodramatizing. The quarrels, however, were serious and hard words were exchanged.

> 'Just down for breakfast, sir? You're good enough
> To honour us by coming down at ten!
> Don't fidget, boy. Attention when I speak!
> As I was saying – now I look at you –
> Bone-lazy, like my eldest brother Jack,
> A rotten, low, deceitful little snob.
> Yes, I'm in trade and proud of it, I am!'
> Black waves of hate went racing round the room . . .

His mother knew that they were both in the wrong. The oblivious-ness of youth meant that Betjeman could feel no sense of responsibility himself until much later. When his father died, however, he was unable to eat for several days. This oppressive sense of guilt has manifested itself in several poems.

While at Marlborough, Betjeman suffered one of those crises of faith to which boys in those days were prone and he refused to be confirmed. He had come to find the public-school version of Christianity, as a sort of stiff upper lip of the soul, unbearable. Betjeman was a romantic, in religion as in all things, and he wanted a faith which made an aesthetic as well as a spiritual appeal. He has said many times that he fears his wavering belief – Anglo-agnosti-cism, as he calls it – has its origin in love of worship for its own sake, incense and candles, and, above all, church architecture, rather than in deep spiritual conviction. He has hope rather than faith. His adolescent doubts were, to some extent, allayed by an eccentric Cornish clergyman encountered on one of his architectural rambles who recognized the nature of the boy's doubts and lent him Arthur Machen's *The Secret Glory*, a highly coloured, romantic book, heavy with Celtic mysticism. It was, nevertheless, refreshing after the dull orthodoxies with which he had been force-fed at school and he welcomed it as such. It also reassured him that his sense of isolation was not unique.

He was, of course, lonely, like most imaginative schoolboys in large and rowdy schools, and his adolescent desires were projected on to the handsome athletes who did not notice him. This lack of love deepened his sense of isolation and doom. Almost at the end of his school career, however, he established a platonic friendship with another boy very different from himself, a hearty games-player who was 'mad on cars'. This brief infatuation served to irradiate Marlborough in his final term:

> I was released
> Into Swinburnian stanzas with the wind.
> I felt so strong that I could leap a brook,
> So clever, I could master anything;
> For Marlborough now was home and beautiful.

Loving and being loved, even so pure a love as this, had, as it always does, restored self-esteem and invested the dull routine of daily life with infinite possibilities. At home, there were girls to be taken to dances and Betjeman was always intensely susceptible to female beauty; but this innocent episode of calf-love remained as a never-to-be-forgotten idyll.

In 1925, Betjeman went up to Magdalen College, Oxford, to read English with the Master of Marlborough's advice still ringing in his ears: 'Oxford is a very delightful place. Make sure you don't find it too delightful.' It was advice the hedonistic Betjeman was not inclined to take. Installed in spacious eighteenth-century rooms, the latest novels on his shelves, gold-tipped Balkan Sobranies in the cigarette-box and Tokay and sherry in the cupboard, he could scarcely believe his good fortune.

> Privacy after years of public school;
> Dignity after years of none at all –
> First college rooms, a kingdom of my own:
> What words of mine can tell my gratitude?

He threw himself into a hectic round of parties which boded ill for his success in Schools:

> I cut tutorials with wild excuse,
> For life was luncheons, luncheons all the way –
> And evenings dining with the Georgeoisie.

He spent lavishly on clothes – Charvet ties, expensive suits, handmade shoes – so that the picture of the young exquisite conjured up in *Summoned by Bells* is scarcely recognizable in the crumple-suited figure familiar from more recent television appearances.

Silk-dressing-gowned, to Sunday-morning bells,
Long after breakfast had been cleared in Hall,
I wandered to my lavender-scented bath;
Then, with a loosely knotted shantung tie
And hair well soaked in Delhez' Genêt d'Or,
Strolled to the Eastgate.

Oxford in the twenties has been described time and again in memoirs and diaries with the result that everyone now knows that the University was divided into rival camps of 'aesthetes' and 'hearties', Harold Acton acting as *arbiter elegantiarum* to the aesthetes. Betjeman was a self-confessed aesthete, if a good deal less outrageous than Acton and his friends. His interest in nineteenth-century church architecture, obscure parson poets, the minutiae of ecclesiastical ritual – while capable of being dismissed as, 'My dear, too amusing' – was deep and, at heart, scholarly. Though it might, incidentally, amuse Betjeman and his friends, it was essentially serious and became more so as he grew older. It was a world away from the sort of amateurish interest in Victorian bric à brac – musical boxes, wax fruit under domes, wool-work samplers and the like – affected by Harold Acton and Robert Byron, though some of Betjeman's friends were puzzled by his unusual interests and suspected that they were part of some prolonged joke. But to Maurice Bowra it seemed that, while it may have begun as a joke, 'even then his curiosity was genuinely aroused and he found a real excitement in it. Later, despite all his jokes, it was serious and he really looked for what the Victorian architects were trying to do and discriminated firmly between them and their different abilities and accomplishments. The Victorian age appealed to something deep in him. Its security, its religion, its sense of social order were what he wanted for his own happiness and in it he found an unlimited field for his lively and enquiring mind.'

Betjeman was enchanted by Oxford. He wanted to escape from the respectable, bourgeois world of his parents and to this end he cultivated the rich, the fashionable, the titled.

I soon left Old Marlburians behind.
(As one more solemn of our number said:
'Spiritually I was at Eton, John')

He visited country houses such as Sezincote in Gloucestershire – a

Hindu pleasure-dome in Cotswold stone and forerunner of the Brighton Pavilion. Ironically, it was in this exotic setting that he first met Clement Attlee, a politician for whom he always had warm feelings.

> Oxford May mornings! When the prunus bloomed
> We'd drive to Sunday lunch at Sezincote:
> First steps in learning how to be a guest,
> First wood-smoke-scented luxury of life
> In the large ambience of a country house.

He became a bosom friend of the Marquess of Dufferin and Ava and stayed, during vacations, at his great house at Clandeboye in Ulster, visits which nurtured his love of Ireland, Irish eighteenth-century architecture and the families of the Anglo-Irish ascendancy. He was taken up by the immensely rich Edward James and was a frequent luncheon guest in the beautifully furnished rooms he occupied in Canterbury Quad. Bowra has said that Betjeman liked the peerage because it was 'anomalous and unusual' rather than because he entertained romantic notions about it, as Evelyn Waugh did. He was certainly amused and fascinated by the eccentricities which thrived in aristocratic families but he also took a sensual delight in luxury and privilege, as the extract from *Summoned by Bells* shows.

John Dugdale, whose family owned Sezincote, was a socialist, as of course was Hugh Gaitskell, who had come up to Oxford at about the same time. Despite his friends, Betjeman's interest in socialism never went very deep. Though, after leaving Oxford, he went so far as to buy *Das Kapital*, he later confessed that he 'could never get beyond the first two paragraphs'. He has said that he also took a left-wing newspaper called *Workers' Weekly* because he liked to be seen reading it on buses and trains. When the General Strike occurred during his time at Oxford, he 'felt obliged to be in sympathy with the strikers', largely out of consideration for the views of these socialist friends. His polite offers to carry messages for the N.U.R. at Didcot were, unfortunately, turned down by the railwaymen. During the early thirties, he became interested in Conrad Noel, the so-called 'Red Vicar' of Thaxted, and his ideas. It was a time when socialism cropped up in the most unlikely places. Noel himself was a spiritual heir of William Morris and believed that joy could be re-introduced to the lives of men and women if they took up handicrafts. Betjeman was fascinated by him as a character though he had been inclined to regard the 'arts and crafts' movement as something of a joke. Perhaps, his interest in socialism was more of a pose than any of his other interests. Certainly it was very shortlived.

As well as friendships with peers, millionaires and well-heeled socialists, Betjeman also made friends with Wystan Auden, then occupying permanently shuttered rooms in Canterbury Quad. They shared an interest in church architecture and minor nineteenth-century poets, such as the Reverend E. E. Bradford, whose work they liked to recite over tea. As well as Auden, Betjeman also kept up with Louis MacNeice, Bernard Spencer and John Bowle, all of them old Marlborough friends. It was with Auden and MacNeice that he helped write one of the shortest, and oddest, erotic verses in the language:

> I often think that I would like
> To be the saddle of a bike.

He remained on friendly terms with Auden and MacNeice through-out their lives. With Auden, in particular, he had a peculiar affinity. In spite of his cosmopolitanism and omnivorous interest in European culture, Auden was always something of a little Englander. His love of the English landscape was as deep as Betjeman's, though less exclusive, and, towards the end of his life, he became, like Betjeman, a devout Anglo-Catholic. It was Auden who first encouraged Betjeman to go to the Isle of Man. Appropriately, one of their last meetings was 'in the Refreshment Room of the Great Central Railway on Marylebone Station, before it was ruined by redecora-tion', for Auden shared Betjeman's love of railways and had an almost equally encyclopaedic knowledge of Bradshaw.

As well as dining out, entertaining (he invented a cocktail, consisting of equal parts sherry and advocaat, which he says tasted like 'liquid cake'), indulging his taste for titles and country-house life and buying expensive clothes, Betjeman was running up vast bills for books at Blackwell's – bills which he did not settle until his father died in 1932 – and writing poems for the delectation of a select audience. For a while, he edited *Cherwell*, the more scurrilous of the two undergraduate papers. He was also a member of OUDS but, owing to a ribald caption which he attached to a photograph of them rehearsing, he was declared *persona non grata* by Harman

Grisewood and expelled from the cast of *King Lear* in which he was
to play the Fool in Komisarjevsky's production.

According to Osbert Lancaster, another contemporary at Oxford,
despite his Sulka shirts and Charvet ties, Betjeman appeared to be
making 'a sustained and successful effort to present a convincing
impersonation of a rather down-at-heel Tractarian hymn-writer
recently unfrocked' at this time. His slightly woebegone appearance,
strangely at odds with the expensive clothes, appealed to women,
with whom Betjeman enjoyed considerable success. Some of his
romances expired in typically bizarre fashion, as when a waitress of
whom he was fond ('Olive Sparks. Eton crop. Very nice') offended
him by doing the foxtrot in the aisle of Gloucester Cathedral.
Another had to be despatched because she acquired a 'particularly
unbecoming' mackintosh.

At Oxford, Betjeman also found his way back to the Church. The
love of ritual which had been implanted in him by Arthur Machen's
book found ample fulfilment in the splendour of Anglican worship at
Pusey House, that shrine of Anglo-Catholicism which kept alive the
spirit of the Oxford Movement. It was at Pusey House that he was
confirmed and there he could indulge to the full his love of incense,
candles, and high church ritual at its most flamboyant. He went
regularly to confession and communion, usually after a late breakfast:

> Oxford marmalade
> And a thin volume by Lowes Dickinson
> But half-engaged my thoughts till Sunday calm
> Led me by crumbling walls and echoing lanes,
> Past college chapels with their organ-groan
> And churches stacked with bicycles outside,
> To worship at High Mass in Pusey House.

There is something slightly distasteful about this mixture of
sophisticated insouciance ('But half-engaged my thoughts . . .') and
Christian worship. It was almost as if, for Betjeman, attendance at
church was just another aesthetic experience, a source of pleasure,
like dining at the George, rather than the fulfilment of a deep
spiritual need. Betjeman has, of course, never denied that his
Christian belief was aroused by the love of architecture and elaborate
ritual. But, though his faith has continued to be shaky, he remains
convinced 'that the one fundamental thing is that Christ was God'
and 'really I don't think life would be worth living if it weren't

true'. Whilst architecture and ritual are sources of pleasure – why should they not be? – as well as aids to belief, he knows that they are nothing beside this one essential fact. Through all his doubts and backslidings, he has tried to keep this one central idea before him.

There has always been an apparent contradiction between Betjeman's style of living – epicurean, hedonistic, extravagant, carried on among the rich and famous – and his intellectual and imaginative taste for the dim, the obscure, the neglected; for non-conformist chapels, suburban railways, minor nineteenth-century poets, Victorian architecture. At Oxford, this must have seemed particularly bizarre. It was this apparent contradiction, one assumes, which made Betjeman so attractive a companion to such men as Maurice Bowra, a highly intelligent man who, as a don, was able to pick and choose among his undergraduate acquaintances. From the outset, he acknowledged Betjeman's uniqueness: 'Betjeman has a mind of extraordinary originality; there is no one else remotely like him.'

Bowra was one of the great Oxford characters. At his dinner table ('I'm a man more dined against than dining' was one of his better-known *bon mots*), he would hold forth brilliantly and wittily: declaiming modern poetry, pouring scorn on academic hacks and industrious mediocrities. It was Bowra who introduced Betjeman to the poetry of Tennyson and Hardy, both major influences on his own work, and Betjeman has never tried to conceal his debt.

> I learned,
> If learn I could, how not to be a bore,
> And merciless was his remark that touched
> The tender spot if one were showing off.
> Within those rooms I met my friends for life.
> True values there were handed on a plate
> As easily as sprouts and aubergines . . .

Bowra represented true scholarship for Betjeman. He was a man for whom learning was not just the dry-as-dust accumulation of degrees in order to scale the pyramids of worldly success, but a life-enhancing and humane pursuit, one of life's pleasures.

> King of a kingdom underneath the stars,
> I wandered back to Magdalen, certain then,
> As now, that Maurice Bowra's company
> Taught me far more than all my tutors did.

Although never a member of 'Sligger' Urquhart's famous set – unlike his contemporaries Cyril Connolly, Kenneth Clark and Anthony Powell – he was particularly fond of another don, G. A. Kolkhorst, Reader in Spanish and Portuguese, who had a rival salon. Kolkhorst was nicknamed 'the Colonel' because he 'looked so little like one'. According to Osbert Lancaster, he was 'highly ridiculous, but dearly loved'. His whole manner exuded the spirit of the nineties and, indeed, he had been a friend of Pater's and kept his photograph in his rooms. Betjeman enjoyed shocking the old exquisite with rowdy renditions of ballads of his own composition, like 'D'ye ken Kolkhorst' to the tune of 'John Peel', when attending sherry parties in his rooms in Beaumont Street. Betjeman, in fact, had a remarkable gift for improvisation of this sort. Lord David Cecil has recalled that when they were both out together and decided to go and have afternoon tea, Betjeman suddenly burst out with some apposite lines to the tune of 'Three Blind Mice':

> Home-made cakes! home-made cakes!
> Dainty buttered scones! dainty buttered scones!
> All served up by gentle-folk
> On beautiful tables of polished oak
> Wherever we went we always spoke
> For home-made cakes . . .

Whilst Bowra was fun but also a scholar, Kolkhorst was just fun, with the result that

> No one believed you really were a don
> Till Gerard Irvine (now a parish priest)
> Went to your lecture on *Le Cid* and clapped.
> You swept towards him, gowned, and turned him out.

For his own tutor at Magdalen, however, Betjeman's feelings were a good deal less affectionate. C. S. Lewis was precisely the kind of man – earnest, pipe-smoking, essentially humourless – Betjeman found least sympathetic. Lewis came to occupy a place in his gallery of *bêtes noires* similar to that of C. R. M. Cruttwell, the Dean of Hertford, in Evelyn Waugh's. Had Betjeman been a novelist, there would undoubtedly have been a succession of obnoxious minor characters sharing the name 'Lewis', just as there is a succession of odious 'Crutwells' in Evelyn Waugh's early novels.

As it is, there are not a few slighting references to Lewis in Betjeman's own early writing. In the introduction to his *Shell Guide to Devon* (1936), for instance, Betjeman wrote: 'For mental inspiration, the Editor had only to think of Mr C. S. Lewis, tweed-clad and jolly, to get busy with his pen.' In *Continual Dew* (1937), he is thanked 'for the fact on page 256' though there is, of course, no page 256 in the book. It is, perhaps, only fair to point out that Lewis was not considered unsympathetic by everyone. He was a fine scholar – *The Allegory of Love* is a masterpiece of its kind – and, though his particular brand of Christian apologetics is not to everyone's taste, it seems that he was a warm and humane man. A friend and admirer of Betjeman's of a younger generation, Kingsley Amis, has paid particular tribute to the brilliance of Lewis's lectures. Betjeman, nevertheless, loathed him and Lewis, it must be said, certainly returned the feeling.

In January 1927 he attended a party in Betjeman's elegant rooms in St Aldate's and noted in his diary that he found himself 'pitchforked into a galaxy of super undergraduates' including John Sparrow and Louis MacNeice (of whom Betjeman said, to Lewis's apparent amazement, 'He doesn't say much, but he's a great poet'). Lewis was appalled by their vanity and pretentiousness: 'The conversation was chiefly about lace curtains, arts and crafts (which they all dislike), china ornaments, silver versus earthen teapots, architecture and the strange habits of "hearties". The best thing was Betjeman's curious collection of books.' Lewis's entry concludes ominously, 'Came away with Betjeman to pull him along through Wulfstan until dinner time.'

It was, without doubt, Betjeman's total lack of industry which irked Lewis; he considered him an 'idle prig', too fond of enjoying himself and spending money. In this, perhaps, Betjeman may have detected something of his father. His slackness was indeed legendary, even by the standards of the time. Having found Anglo-Saxon too much for him, he decided to abandon English and take a degree in Welsh. Alas, with no success; though, according to Osbert Lancaster, his disappointment 'was partially compensated for by the knowledge that Magdalen had been put to all the trouble and expense of importing a don from Aberystwyth twice a week, first class' to teach him. In fact, Betjeman was finally sent down having failed in Divinity moderations – then a compulsory, if simple, examination – without a degree.

Not surprisingly, he was downcast at the thought of being banished from his Elysium in such circumstances:

> Failed in Divinity! Oh count the hours
> Spent on my knees in Cowley, Pusey House,
> St Barnabas', St Mary Mag's, St Paul's
> Revering chasubles and copes and albs!
> Consider what I knew of 'High' and 'Low' . . .

Although this might sound rather exaggerated and slightly histrionic, his disappointment was genuine enough. He continues in the same vein:

> I'd seen myself a don,
> Reading old poets in the library,
> Attending chapel in an M.A. gown
> And sipping vintage port by candlelight.

Lewis was unmoved by such daydreams, telling him curtly, when Betjeman sought him out 'in his arid room': 'You'd have only got a Third.'

So Betjeman left Oxford, where he had been happy and made so many friends, with the unattractive prospect of going into the family firm looming before him:

> Pentonville Road! How could I go by tram
> In suit from Savile Row and Charvet tie?
> How could I, after Canterbury Quad,
> My peers and country houses and my jokes,
> Talk about samples, invoices and stock?

There was more, however, to Betjeman's conviction that he must avoid working in his father's business than snobbery and fastidiousness; just as there was more to him than Lewis realized. From the earliest age, he had known that he 'must be a poet'. This belief in his own talent had now been endorsed by men such as Bowra, whose opinion was worth having. He knew that to fall in with his father's wishes would have robbed him of his independence and of any chance he might have of becoming a writer. (Just how disappointed his father was, in fact, remains uncertain, although Betjeman has continued to feel guilty.) Instead, he did a variety of jobs – secretary to an Irish senator, clerk in an insurance company – as well as making for the 'welcome door' of Gabbitas, Thring and

Co., one of the scholastic agencies in Sackville Street which had secured positions for, among others, Evelyn Waugh and Graham Greene. Greene has written that to the young men of his generation down from university, 'recourse to Sackville Street was like recourse to the pawnshop in earlier days . . . You pawned yourself instead of your watch.' With no degree, the best they could offer Betjeman was a post as cricket master, though he knew nothing about cricket, at a preparatory school in Bucks. He recounts his bizarre experiences at this school in his poem, 'Cricket Master', a sort of postscript to *Summoned by Bells*. Though he was popular with the boys, presumably because he was easy-going and made them laugh, the other masters regarded him as a frivolous impostor and not without reason. He enjoyed his time as a schoolmaster but, despite Evelyn Waugh's warning that he 'would never laugh so much again', he abandoned it, willingly enough, for a job, obtained through Maurice Bowra's influence, on the *Architectural Review* in 1931.

This magazine, the most sumptuous and prestigious of architectural magazines, was then nominally edited by Christian Barman and had its offices in an eighteenth-century house in Queen Anne's Gate. Betjeman was installed in a small room, covered in William Morris wallpaper, on the top floor. Here, says Osbert Lancaster, 'he devoted himself to the rehabilitation of C. F. A. Voysey . . . and tireless advocacy of the merits of Norman Shaw'. In this, however, he is mistaken, for Betjeman, though he had discovered that Voysey was still alive and had gone to interview him in his flat over Rumpelmeyer's restaurant, spoke slightingly of Norman Shaw and the 'Queen Anne' style in his book, *Ghastly Good Taste*, published in 1933. He revised this opinion when the book was reissued in 1970, explaining in a footnote that he now considers Norman Shaw 'our greatest architect since Wren, if not greater'. But certainly he was no admirer of his work during those early days on the *Architectural Review*. His major contribution was rather the re-assessment of the architects who were part of the 'arts and crafts' movement and about whom he had previously been so patronizing.

He also wrote articles with titles like 'The Death of Modernism', as well as reviews and *Country Life*-type descriptions of houses in which he had stayed. He was never taken in by what Osbert Lancaster called 'that Bauhaus balls', then the rage. What interested him was not architecture in the abstract, still less abstract architecture, but buildings in their social and physical settings, aspects of the world in which human beings lived: architecture was the background to our lives; a humane art, not a drab science or a matter of aesthetics and pure form as preached in the academies. He had no sympathy for Le Corbusier's famous dictum that a house is 'a machine for living'. Though he was not above trying to seem smart and doctrinaire when it suited him ('wanting to be up to date but really preferring all centuries to my own'), his real sympathies were with architecture which pleased the eye and, for the most part, this meant the architecture of the past.

He also began to publish stories and poems in other magazines, notably the *London Mercury* (in which 'Death in Leamington' appeared in 1930). In 1929, he wrote a curious short story, 'Lord Mount Prospect', about an undergraduate Society for the Discovery of Obscure Peers which sets off in pursuit of the eponymous peer. It is an amusing and eccentrically original piece which piquantly combines Betjeman's taste for the peerage, for Irish country houses and for the oddities of non-conformity. Despite its air of having been written for the amusement of a handful of friends who knew of his interest in such things, it found a place in Gollancz's *Great Stories of Detection, Mystery and Horror* in 1934.

The editor of the *London Mercury* was J. C. Squire, the very model of a modern Georgian poet. He was regarded as hopelessly philistine by the literary *beau monde*, particularly by the Sitwells, though he was a talented and versatile writer. Betjeman got on well with him and joined with him in campaigns to save bits of London which, even then, were being threatened by the developers. It was through Squire that Betjeman met Eric Gillett who suggested the striking title which Betjeman gave to his first prose book, *Ghastly Good Taste*. This book was published by Chapman and Hall, whose managing director was Evelyn Waugh's father. By the time it appeared, Betjeman had indisputably gained himself a toe-hold in the literary world.

His early poems had earned him a small but enthusiastic following and one of his earliest admirers, Edward James, a friend from Oxford, had printed a small selection of his verse called *Mount Zion* in 1931. In fact, Betjeman was living in a house – 'small, luxurious, with limewood walls and pale carpets' – in Culross Street which James owned. He shared it with Randolph Churchill, whose legendary uproariousness must have tried even Betjeman's patience. Churchill was another early admirer of Betjeman's poems and gladly undertook the job of correcting the galley proofs of *Mount Zion*. Betjeman has recalled how he 'used to make me recite the stuff at lunch parties, and at dinners, he used to ask for special favourites and then listen with his eyes wide open, and laughter in his face, and lead applause at the end'. He also used to offer Betjeman money to persuade him to write. It was to be some time, however, before he became something more than the toast of a small circle of friends.

While working on the *Architectural Review* Betjeman met Penelope Hester Chetwode, the daughter of Field Marshal Lord Chetwode, the Commander-in-Chief in India, whom he was to marry in 1933. Their courtship was not an easy one as her family strongly disapproved of Betjeman's bourgeois origins. Her mother is supposed to have said: 'We ask people like that to our houses, but we don't marry them'; a remark, as John Press observed, worthy of Lady Bracknell. Maurice Bowra said that the Field Marshal found it difficult to remember Betjeman's foreign-sounding name and told the butler, after their marriage, that his daughter was no longer to be addressed as Miss Penelope but as 'Mrs Bargeman'.

Betjeman was in no way put off by the high-handedness of his prospective parents-in-law. Osbert Lancaster recalled, in a *Sunday Times* profile of Betjeman, that the Chetwodes 'gave a white-tie dinner at the Savoy to mark the event. John went to amazing pains to get a made-up tie sewn on elastic. Throughout the dinner, he plucked the bow forward six or seven inches and let it snap back – purely to annoy his future mother-in-law.' Betjeman was never a sycophant. His aristocratic friends were expected to accept him on his own terms. He never tried to disguise himself in tweeds, as Evelyn Waugh did, or ride to hounds. He says he still feels hopelessly middle class.

Penelope was (and, of course, still is) as original and eccentric as her husband. Her beauty, wit and dynamic energy entranced his friends. She was a passionate horsewoman, an excellent cook, a devotee of Indian art and architecture – he met her, in fact, as a result of an article on the Rock Temples of Ellora which she submitted to the *Architectural Review*. She also became an intrepid traveller and has published two superb travel books: *Kulu*, and *Two Middle-Aged Ladies in Andalusia* in which her companion was a horse.

After their marriage, they rented Garrard's Farm at Uffington in

Berkshire, for which they paid thirty-six pounds a year. They both enjoyed village life and Penelope took to lecturing the local Women's Institute on subjects such as Indian mysticism, Nepalese temple architecture and the making of mayonnaise, not then a commonplace sight at village dinner tables. Sometimes the villagers would be invited to the house for impromptu musical recitals. Osbert Lancaster has recorded an occasion when the villagers had been asked to bring home-made wine to one of these sessions: 'The principal item on the programme was a performance of "Sumer is icumen in" sung by Adrian Bishop, Bowra, my wife and the poet himself, accompanied on the piano by Lord Berners, and by Penelope on a strange instrument resembling a zither. So powerful was the effect that all present remained rooted to their seats even when, as happened from time to time, a home-made bottle exploded, showering those in the immediate vicinity with broken glass and elderberry juice.' Auden also visited them and wrote some lines for the village play which Penelope was producing.

From the first, however, the marriage was a stormy one; hardly surprising with two such volatile and independent personalities. There were frequent, violent quarrels and, despite the fact that they had two children, a boy and a girl, Betjeman always maintained his separate life in London. He has said that he always regarded his wife as 'the possessor of my children, not me'. Though his friends have meant much to him, he has never been a family man in the usual sense of the term.

Betjeman had left the *Architectural Review* in 1933, the year of his marriage. In 1935 he joined his friends Randolph Churchill and Patrick Balfour on the *Evening Standard*. He had attracted Beaverbrook's attention by the piece he had written on obscure peers and was taken on as a film critic with instructions to praise everything. Malcolm Muggeridge was editing the 'Londoner's Diary' at the same time and recalls that Betjeman, in addition to films, 'helped out with architectural and ecclesiastical news, especially clerical appointments'. This was certainly more to his taste than film criticism, of which he understood nothing. By far the most interesting thing about the job was the opportunity it afforded of meeting attractive film stars. When he interviewed Myrna Loy, he persuaded her to let him say that she was 'very interested' in English Perpendicular architecture, a confession which must have convulsed his friends even if it mystified most of his readers. The enjoyment

he took in all this is summed up in a couplet he wrote after taking
a young starlet from Gainsborough Films to lunch:

> I sit inside the Cheshire Cheese
> With Gainsborough Girl upon my knees.

Enjoyable as it was, however, he was sacked after only a few
months.

Throughout the thirties he did an immense amount of journalism,
including book reviews and occasional architectural criticism. He
also lectured extensively and began to appear on wireless and
television, then in its infancy, talking usually about architecture or
topographical subjects. As well as dabbling in documentary film
work, he was also signed up to write advertising copy for Shell
Petroleum by Jack Beddington, the firm's publicity manager,
described by Peter Quennell as a 'modern Maecenas . . . who
allocated a monthly fee to any writer or artist he considered worth
encouraging'. Betjeman enjoyed the discipline imposed by this sort
of work, in which every word had to pull its weight. He also edited
the Shell Guides – for *Cornwall* (1934) and *Devon* (1936) – which
the company were producing as motorists' handy gazetteers of the
English counties. In addition, he was publishing poems in metropolitan reviews and magazines as well as in obscure parish magazines, and in extremely limited editions issued from private presses.
(For instance, his ballad *Sir John Piers* appeared in Ireland in 1938 in
an edition of only one hundred and forty copies under the Huxleyan
pseudonym 'Epsilon'.) His second collection of poems, *Continual
Dew*, was brought out by Murray, the firm which has published all
subsequent volumes of his poetry, in 1937. Although more of a
commercial venture than *Mount Zion*, its reception – Peter Quennell
spoke of its deliciously 'tasteful tastelessness' in his review in the
New Statesman – suggested that Betjeman was still regarded as a
clever and witty freak rather than as a serious poet. Though he
could be relished as an original, remarkable for his off-beat
sensibility, it seemed ridiculous to take him too seriously. He was
an interesting tributary rather than part of the mainstream. It was
only later that this erroneous view began to be corrected.

When war broke out in 1939, Betjeman, being rather old for
active service, sought work in a civilian capacity. He started out in
the Films Division of the Ministry of Information. His most
interesting appointment was as United Kingdom Press Attaché in

Dublin from 1941 to 1943, though he later worked in a secret department of the Admiralty ('What did I do? God knows') as well as in the Books Section of the British Council, then housed in hutments in the park at Blenheim. In these jobs Betjeman revealed unexpected talents for administration. Although the post in Dublin was a particularly sensitive and difficult one because of Ireland's parlous neutrality, Betjeman was an enormous success and with his chief, Sir John Maffey, did much to foster Anglo-Irish cultural relations. He did not, however, forsake personal eccentricity and insisted on dating all minutes according to the liturgical calendar. He befriended Irish writers and was encouraged by John Lehmann to persuade them to submit pieces for his magazine, *New Writing*. He also saw a lot of Geoffrey Taylor, with whom he worked on *Time and Tide*, who was editing *The Bell*, the Irish equivalent of *Horizon*. He joined the Kildare Street Club, the inner sanctum of the Anglo-Irish ascendancy, and he and Penelope – who accompanied him with her Arab horse, Moti – were able to see their Irish friends frequently. Betjeman had always loved Ireland and he decided to take the opportunity to learn Erse; he even took to signing his letters 'Sean O'betjeman'. It was a 'good' war in every sense of the word.

He continued to write. As well as *Old Lights for New Chancels* (1940), which added greatly to his poetic stature, he published among other things two topographical works, *Vintage London* (1942) and *English Cities and Small Towns* (1943), an attractive essay in Collins' Britain in Pictures series, designed to deepen the people's understanding of the national heritage they were being asked to fight for. In addition, he wrote a monograph on the painter *John Piper* (1944) who, with his wife, Myfanwy, had become one of Betjeman's closest friends following their collaborations on the Shell Guides. Piper shared all Betjeman's tastes and interests and after the war they edited a number of guide books together – Murray's Architectural Guides for *Buckinghamshire* (1948) and *Berkshire* (1949), as well as the *Shell Guide to Shropshire* (1951) – which afforded them wonderful opportunities to visit out-of-the-way churches and villages at their publishers' expense. John Piper and Osbert Lancaster are the ideal illustrators of Betjeman's work. In fact, the three men have remarkably compatible talents; some of Osbert Lancaster's drawings of Byzantine churches being very Piperesque, his brilliant series of books – *Progress at Pelvis Bay,*

Pillar to Post and *Homes Sweet Homes* – being a sort of continuation of *Ghastly Good Taste*. Similarly, Betjeman's *vers de société* might be regarded as the literary equivalent of the pocket cartoon.

In 1945, Betjeman published his second wartime collection of verse, *New Bats in Old Belfries*. This book continued the movement away from the frivolity of the earlier collections. Goronwy Rees, who reviewed it in the *Spectator*, thought he detected 'an increasing mellowness and an increasing seriousness' in Betjeman's work and concluded by saying that 'his poems are both clever and good, and perhaps as they become less clever they become even better'. The cautious 'perhaps' suggests that Rees may have felt that he was sticking his neck out too far in suggesting that Betjeman might be a serious poet rather than a mere entertainer. Even so, it was a sign that people were beginning to re-assess Betjeman. Auden produced his selection from the poetry and prose with an enthusiastic and complimentary introduction in 1947; John Sparrow in his selection of 1948 made an impressive case for Betjeman as a serious topo-graphical poet in the tradition of Crabbe and Cowper. *Selected Poems* was a great popular success and won Betjeman the Heinemann Award for Literature. In the space of a decade, he had ceased to be the darling of a clique and had become common property.

After the war, Betjeman continued to write regularly for news-papers and magazines. He had previously worked for *Night and Day* – the shortlived magazine which expired in 1937 as a result of a libel suit brought against Graham Greene, the magazine's film critic, by Shirley Temple – to which he contributed a lively column called 'Percy Progress'. He now worked for the eccentric Lady Rhondda's magazine, *Time and Tide*, though he was eventually sacked; an incident commemorated in his poem 'Caprice'. In 1952, a job was secured for him as book reviewer on the *Daily Telegraph* by a relative of his wife. While he has often been sacked, Betjeman has never been short of people who could pull strings. He has never thought very highly of his journalism – even the delightful weekly column which he contributed to the *Spectator* – saying, 'I was never much cop as a journalist, hated news, could only write prissy little pieces – the effect of sunlight on leaves.' He has been happy to write for papers such as the *Daily Express*, finding it more lucrative and less demanding then writing for 'serious' journals such as the *New Statesman* (or *Stateswoman*, as he likes to call it) which he thinks pretentious and dull, 'always putting you in your place'. During

Malcolm Muggeridge's editorship, he was a frequent guest at the *Punch* table but, though his presence certainly enlivened these gatherings, he contributed relatively little to the magazine itself.

Broadcasting began to take up more and more of his time. He had been, for instance, an early member of the Brains Trust, both on wireless and television. These portentous programmes were filmed with the 'brains' sitting round a table having apparently just finished a meal. The studio was got up to look like a room and Malcolm Muggeridge recalls Betjeman, on one occasion, exposing the deception by suddenly seizing one of the plastic logs in the grate and waving it about expressively in order to emphasize a point. Clearly, Betjeman was, as they say, a 'natural'. His television appearances were to become an important part of his life and work and have certainly helped foster his unique relationship with the reading public.

During these years, Betjeman and his wife were living in an old rectory at Wantage in Berkshire: a large red-brick Victorian family house which provided ample shelter for Betjeman's books and his wife's horses. When Evelyn Waugh stayed with them in October 1946 he repaid their hospitality in characteristic fashion by writing an unkind, if amusing, description of the ménage in his diary:

> In the late afternoon to stay with the Betjemans in a lightless, stuffy, cold, poky rectory among beechwoods overlooking Wantage. Harness everywhere. A fine collection of nineteenth-century illustrated books. Delicious food cooked by Penelope. I brought sherry, burgundy, port. A daughter of grossly proletarian appearance and manner.

Waugh had been a friend of Betjeman's since the twenties and he was particularly fond of Penelope, to whom he dedicated his novel *Helena* in 1950. It was during the late forties that he began to address a barrage of letters to Betjeman in an attempt to browbeat him into giving up his, to Waugh, absurd Anglo-Catholicism and coming over to Rome. Waugh grounds his argument on logic and completely refuses to allow for Betjeman's emotional loyalties to the Church of England. 'It is no good,' he writes, 'saying: "I don't happen to be logical." Logic is simply the architecture of human reason. If you try to base your life on logical absurdities YOU WILL GO MAD . . . Your ecclesiastical position is entirely without reason. You cannot

possibly be right. Marxist-Atheists might be. Zealous protestants
may be . . .' He goes on to inform Betjeman that there is no more
resemblance between Anglo-Catholics and Roman Catholics than
between 'a piece of Trust House timbering and a genuine Tudor
building', the kind of comparison that might have been expected to
weigh with one of Betjeman's architectural turn of mind. Waugh
asserts dogmatically: 'The True Church is unique and indivisible
and nothing is remotely like it. This may not be apparent from
outside. But I think more violence is done to the Mystical Body by
those who imitate it than by those who frankly hate it.' As well as
believing that he was endangering his immortal soul, Waugh
thought that Betjeman's religious faith was a compound of sloppy
sentiment and woolly-mindedness. It was not built, like his own,
on the solid foundation of reason but on the shifting sands of
emotion. Waugh seems never to have entertained a doubt in his life
and his friend's legitimate doubts were dismissed as 'the natural
eruptions of a thoroughly bad intellectual constitution'. He goes
on, in fine dogmatic style, to say: 'If you accept an absurdity, as you
do in pretending the church of Wantage is the Catholic Church, and
luxuriate in sentimental raptures, you will naturally break out in
boils and carbuncles and question the authenticity of the Incarnation.'

Despite having been accused of sentimentality, illogicality and
threatened with madness and visitations of boils, Betjeman stood
his ground. He replied that he could not believe that 'the Church of
England is not part of the Catholic Church'. Waugh was, nevertheless, unprepared to let go. He recognized the sacrifice Betjeman
would be making but urged him to seek instruction at Farm Street:
'Almost everyone who becomes a Catholic makes sacrifices. Some
very large ones. Yours I think would be greater than most for you
have built your life around the Church of England. I can well
understand your reluctance to start a new life in middle age with
every literary and aesthetic predilection the other way. It is easy to
say, "Well I'll just wait until an Archangel is sent to make the
announcement to me personally in God's good time. Meanwhile,
I'll believe in the Incarnation on two days a week and continue my
catalogue of Anglican churches." ' He concluded by putting four
clear-cut propositions for Betjeman to ponder: '(1) We may both be
wrong. (2) We can't both be right. (3) You cannot be right and I
wrong. (4) If I am right you are wrong. Which of these statements

do you deny? A real protestant could deny (3), but your Wantage waifs don't and can't.' Betjeman replied, rather limply, that: 'All I can do now is to read, pray and study the life of Our Lord. That I am doing. I feel that it is not so much a matter of which church as of loving God and I still think of us *both* as right.' It was not in Betjeman's character to be as certain of anything as Waugh appeared to be of everything.

Waugh's concern was genuine enough even if his language and arguments appeared unsympathetic and uncompromising. He liked and admired Betjeman and wanted him to embrace the Truth as he saw it. He succeeded only in upsetting him deeply, both because of his hectoring tone and, more importantly, because his proselytizing seemed to be having more effect on Betjeman's wife than on him. She wrote to Waugh in June 1948, apropos his hortatory letters to her husband and her own imminent conversion to Rome, that 'he [Betjeman] is in a dreadful state he thinks you are the devil and wakes up in the middle of the night and raves and says he will leave me if I go over . . . He thinks *Roman* Catholicism is a foreign religion which has no right to set up in this country, let alone try to make converts from what he regards as the true Catholic church of the country. Your letters have brought it out in a remarkable way.'

In fact, for Betjeman it was the Englishness of Anglo-Catholicism as much as the Catholicism which was important. The Church was not just a series of dogmas to which reason demanded assent but a social and spiritual entity rooted in the English soil. He regarded it as a social as well as a spiritual duty to maintain his connection with it. It was the national religion and, as such, demanded his allegiance and loyalty. He had written to Waugh that in his village 'the only bulwark against complete paganism is the Church and its chief supporters are Penelope and me . . . In villages people still follow a lead.' He believed that to desert what he thought was the Catholic church in England would be a betrayal not only of his own beliefs but also an abdication of his responsibility to those of his fellows who could not and would not follow him.

Whether or not Penelope's conversion to Rome was the cause of it, Betjeman's marriage began to deteriorate at about this time. Their shared religion had certainly been an important bond. Now that was gone, there seemed, perhaps, to be little to keep them together. Betjeman had his life in London and his wife had her horses and her house in the country. The family home at Wantage was eventually sold in the early seventies and they have, since then, maintained entirely separate establishments. Betjeman's son, Paul, had decamped to Utah and become a Mormon almost as soon as he left Eton. Betjeman feels that this decision may have been prompted by the awareness that he was in danger of being stultified by his father's fame. His daughter, Candida, however, was more at home in the world her father inhabited and has carved out a name for herself, both as one of the earliest contributors to *Private Eye* and later as an historian of public lavatories and suburban gardens. She is a particularly attractive woman who is married to Mr Rupert Lycett-Green, the owner of Blades. Her own two children are, one imagines, a source of great delight to both Betjeman and his wife; his latest collection of verse is dedicated to them.

Although these post-war years were not particularly happy for Betjeman, they produced some of his finest poems. In *A Few Late Chrysanthemums* (1954), as John Press has said, 'the good poems come so thick and fast that any appraisal of the volume runs the risk of degenerating into a laudatory catalogue'. The book was awarded the Loines Award for Poetry and the Foyle Poetry Prize. The presentation, undertaken by Lord Samuel, turned out, however, to be an occasion of high farce. Samuel was a politician of the art-fancying kind who knew what he liked and liked what he knew. He spoke disparagingly of 'the fashion for deliberate and perverse obscurity' in much modern verse, quoting Dylan Thomas's 'A Grief Ago' in support of his view (which prompted Stephen Spender to walk out) and heralding Betjeman as a welcome return to sanity. Betjeman was presumably embarrassed by all this. He claimed not to know who had written the poem which had been quoted (out of kindness to Lord Samuel, one suspects, rather than genuine ignorance).

He might have said that difficulty which arises from extreme compression, whether of imagery, emotion or thought is not in itself bad – it is as typical of Donne or Blake as of modern poets such as Thomas – though difficulty which arises from clumsy or muddled thinking is meretricious and deserving of censure. What really matters is sincerity of thought and emotion: a simple, direct poem which is emotionally null and riddled with clichés is as bad as a wilfully obscure one. A reader must make the effort to understand what a poet is trying to say and decide for himself whether he is saying it well. It is fatal to come armed with ready-

made notions of what a poem should be. A sensitive reader should
be constantly on the look-out for new modes of expression and
feeling. That he did not say any of this is, of course, his own affair;
one would expect him to agree with it, none the less.

The incident, trivial and amusing in itself – popular bard praised
by elder statesman, ageing *enfant terrible* exits pursued by pressmen
– illustrates the difficulty of Betjeman's position. He was a serious
poet admired by the sort of people who struck terror and loathing
into serious critics. The irony cannot have been lost on so self-aware
a man as Betjeman. Like the Movement poets who had acquired –
or had thrust upon them – a corporate identity at about the same
time, he preferred clarity to obscurity, tradition to experiment,
poetry which sprang from lived experience rather than from nothing
more than wide reading. He would have shared Larkin's distrust of
'the myth-kitty' and agreed with Amis that 'nobody wants any
more poems about philosophers or paintings or novelists or art
galleries or mythology or foreign cities . . . or at least I hope nobody
wants them'. In this sense, he was more modern than Stephen
Spender who once wrote a poem about Beethoven's death mask or,
for that matter, Dylan Thomas, whose Celtic bardery was rather
suspect in the eyes of these new Augustans.

Betjeman, though apparently unaffected by all that the term
'modernism' implied, was not just an escapist, a traditionalist whose
appeal was, at best, anachronistic. He had married a modern
sensibility to a traditional technique and produced something
genuinely original. His poems are not just the last gasps of a dying
tradition. If they were, they would have only an antiquarian interest;
Betjeman would be no more than a picturesque survival. His
enemies, of course, maintain that he is such a survival; but it is
wrong to think of him in these terms. He stands foursquare in a
tradition of English poetry which is still very much alive. Furthermore, while his poetic models come from the past, he is able to
admire modern poets such as Auden and MacNeice. He is not an
anti-intellectual philistine, unlike so many of his admirers. In fact,
one feels the need occasionally – as one reads Lord Birkenhead's
introduction to the *Collected Poems*, for instance – to protect
Betjeman from his friends.

Despite the popular success of *A Few Late Chrysanthemums*, there
were plenty of hostile critics. This criticism must have hurt
Betjeman, who is a highly sensitive man. Maurice Bowra recalled

the way in which real or imagined slights would sink Betjeman into the blackest misery and the offender be built up into a sort of 'Anti-Christ'; though only to be forgiven a few days later, for he is not a man to bear grudges. He has an unusual talent for friendship to which even people (like John Wain) who do not like his work are not immune. But he is prone to fits of depression which, if anything, have gained in force over the years. He remains a victim of what Churchill called 'the black dog'; feelings of unworthiness and utter futility which are not assuaged by either success or the geniality of his happier moments. He was double-billed with Spike Milligan as one of our leading manic depressives in the *Sunday Times* magazine in 1967.

Despite his personal vulnerability to criticism, Betjeman has fortunately continued to write the only kind of poem which he feels able to. That he has not succumbed to the temptation of being smart or experimental for its own sake is to his credit: he has jumped on no bandwagon, identified himself with no literary clique. He enjoys the public success and recognition which popularity brought but has no illusions about his own importance, preferring to affect an attitude of ironic self-mockery and bemusement. He has no theoretical axe to grind but continues to write about the things which move him in a way that is true to the emotion.

The publication of the *Collected Poems* in 1958 was, of course, an immediate and prodigious success. Though Betjeman did not exactly awake to find himself famous, the process of ceasing to be a minority taste and being recognized as a serious artist, which had begun with the publication of *Selected Poems* and been consolidated by the fine achievement of *A Few Late Chrysanthemums*, was completed with the publication of this book. At last, the range and depth of Betjeman's *oeuvre* was able to be appreciated. Its enormous sales made him something of a phenomenon; sniped at in some quarters and lauded in others. Since its appearance, Betjeman has published two other collections, *High and Low* (1966) and *A Nip in the Air* (1972), as well as a blank verse autobiography, *Summoned by Bells* (1960). None of these productions has added greatly to his stature but nor have they detracted from it. Whilst Betjeman's finest achievement remains the poems of *A Few Late Chrysanthemums*, and the additional poems in the first edition of the *Collected Poems*, he has continued to produce work of a high standard in prose as well as verse.

His television appearances made him a household name, as famous if less notorious than Malcolm Muggeridge. He showed as much talent for the medium as Muggeridge, though nothing of his hypocritical distaste for it. As a broadcaster he was no mere mandarin dispenser of information. In his role of cicerone, whether he was showing the viewers round an old church, a country house, or Queen Victoria's railway carriage, he gave something of himself along with the information so that one watched Betjeman as much as what was on view. Architecture, for Betjeman, was not a subject for academic study but a source of pleasure, even fun, and he managed to communicate this to his audience. He shared his pleasure in what he was seeing and what he said about a building was personal and often humorous rather than drily factual. Furthermore, he saw beauty in things which other people would have ignored – the cast-iron adornments of a Victorian railway station, the decorative ceramic tiles in an Edwardian superstore, the mahogany panelling and velvet upholstery in an old railway carriage – so that he helped create a new way of seeing.

His television appearances in the sixties and seventies became ever more frequent and his success as a 'telly personality' meant that he was expected to do quizzes and chat shows as well as more serious broadcasting. Although this was used as evidence by his detractors that he was no more than a facile entertainer, a mere performer, rather than a real poet, such critics do him an injustice not only as a poet but as a broadcaster as well.

The public success Betjeman has enjoyed – the knighthood, the television fame and, finally, the laureateship – has given him much pleasure. Although he is, in many ways, an intensely private man and one given to deep and unpredictable fits of depression, he is also something of a showman, one who enjoys an audience and the opportunity to play to the gallery. His public persona, his 'Lord Teddy Bear' image, is one that he is conscious of and which he uses professionally. This is, of course, not to say that he is a charlatan. All charmers (and Betjeman certainly has great personal charm) consciously manipulate their talents.

Because of his talents as a broadcaster and his unique popularity as a poet, he has become public property to a far greater extent than is common with writers. The knighthood – which he considers 'useful with restaurants and hotels' – and the laureateship were, in a sense, conferred by the public. The laureateship was a peculiarly appropriate honour and, when his appointment was announced in October 1972, he was overwhelmed with telegrams and congratulatory letters from the sort of people who would not normally mark a literary event. Of course, the laureateship has little enough, as Betjeman is well aware, to do with poetry. There is something rather absurd about the office, with its few guineas a year in lieu of a butt of sack, and its association with poetasters and hangers-on. It is easy to mock it as one of those picturesque survivals so characteristic of 'dear old, bloody old England'. Betjeman, however, has never taken himself too seriously and his genuine reverence for traditional institutions, his love of England, has meant that he is able to enter into the spirit of the office and act as official celebrator in verse of state occasions with unaffected relish. It is true that he has not found it possible to write good poems about such things as the investiture of the Prince of Wales or Princess Anne's wedding or the Queen Mother's eightieth birthday, but he has made honourable and sincere attempts. Although seriously ill, he nevertheless produced a poem to mark the wedding of Prince Charles and Lady Diana Spencer. In fact, one might almost say that if the laureateship had not existed, it would have been necessary to invent it for him.

CHAPTER TWO

LAURELS AND GASLIGHT

There has been a tendency to disparage the poems in Betjeman's two early collections, to dismiss them as mere juvenilia, oddities designed to appeal to a coterie, but this is a mistaken view. To admit the merit of these poems in no way detracts from the qualities of the undoubtedly better work which he produced in the forties and fifties. In fact, those qualities which one admires in the mature Betjeman were present from the start. The tone may be lighter, the rhythms more knockabout, but beneath the comedy there is a pervasive note of melancholy, a depth of feeling and an awareness of the pathos of human life which belies the comic mask.

Nevertheless, the very appearance of these volumes seemed to encourage the view that their contents were mere trifles. *Mount Zion* (1931) was privately printed by Edward James and piles of the slim volumes were stacked in the hall of the house Betjeman was sharing with Randolph Churchill, waiting to be handed out to friends. It was a very private début, Betjeman being something of a collector's item even before many people had heard of him. The book was very prettily got up and was dedicated to Mrs Dugdale, his hostess at Sezincote, in the hope that its preciousness and hyper-sophistication would not alienate her sympathies. *Continual Dew* (1937), although produced by a commercial publisher, maintained this mood of sophisticated amateurism. Though provocatively subtitled *A Little Book of Bourgeois Verse*, it was dedicated to Lord Berners, the multitalented dilettante and near neighbour of Betjeman in Berkshire. It, too, had the look of a ready-made rarity with its prayer-book hinges, top and fore-edge gilding, decorative capitals, woodcuts, engravings, cartoons and sketches by Osbert Lancaster and others, strange surrealist dust-jacket by McKnight Kauffer showing a hand (God's?) emerging from a cabbage, and the punning drawing of a dripping tap on its title page.

Certainly the poems were seen by their early admirers as little more than sophisticated curios. The publisher's blurb for *Continual Dew* emphasizes the gap between Betjeman and the more typical poets of the thirties by referring to him as a *'vieux jeu* verse writer' and mentioning 'a few drawing-room favourites' which have been included from *Mount Zion* (in fact, all the best poems from this collection were included in the new book) 'by special requests'. It goes on to say that 'the verse is nostalgic and designed for those who appreciate Sunday in a provincial town, the subtleties of *high*, *low* and *broad* churchmanship, gaslit London, bottle parties in the suburbs, civil servants on the hike, and half-timbered houses on the southern Electric'. Betjeman enjoyed his reputation for eccentricity and was pleased to be thought of as a picturesque original. This summary of his themes is so sure-footed that it is most likely that he wrote it himself. As he consciously cultivated the role of off-beat entertainer and swimmer against the tide of current literary fashions and practices, he was quite happy to be thought of as a writer of light verse and to take his place in the succession stemming from writers such as Praed and Calverley. In fact, when Auden produced his *Oxford Book of Light Verse* in 1935, Betjeman was the only contemporary whom he included; he also thanked him 'for many valuable suggestions' made during its compilation.

The two poems which Auden chose show, however, how misleading this view could be, even during the thirties. One, 'Westgate-on-Sea', is an unexceptionable choice. Clearly, this picture of a dim Victorian seaside resort with its municipal flowerbeds continually traversed by crocodiles of bespectacled schoolchildren is intended to amuse. Nor is the humour of a particularly sophisticated kind; respectability is mocked in terms which would appeal to a mischievous child. The gentle satire which characterizes the opening lines of the poem is outrageously capped by the ringing absurdity of the last two stanzas:

Church of England bells of Westgate!
  On this balcony I stand,
White the woodwork wriggles round me,
  Clock towers rise on either hand.

For me in my timber arbour
  You have one more message yet,
'Plimsolls, plimsolls in the summer,
  Oh goloshes in the wet!'

The other poem, 'Death of King George V', however, is a much
less obvious choice for such an anthology, even from so idiosyncratic
an editor as Auden. By no stretch of the imagination can it be called
light verse. It is true that the version printed by Auden was
originally called 'Daily Express', because the epigraph ('New King
arrives in his capital by air . . .') was taken from that paper, and that
it contained a facetious topical reference which has now been
removed, but from the first, it was an entirely serious elegy for a
passing world.

Spirits of well-shot woodcock, partridge, snipe
Flutter and bear him up the Norfolk sky:
In that red house in a red mahogany book-case
The stamp collection waits with mounts long dry.

It would be entirely wrong to construe this as mockery of a rather
dull king. Betjeman's tribute is sincere and memorably, even
movingly expressed. The king was a simple but kindly man, his
world was narrow and limited, his pleasures, hunting and shooting,
the typical ones of his class. But Betjeman admires his simplicity
and integrity – 'the big blue eyes' reminiscent of a child's eyes – and
extends his sympathy to the 'old men in country houses' who will
miss him:

Old men who never cheated, never doubted,
Communicated monthly . . .

Against this secure world in which honour, decency and the
Anglican religion were positive forces and not outmoded attitudes
to be mocked at, stands the 'red' new suburb with all its implicit
vulgarity, near which the new king 'lands hatless from the air'.
Betjeman is here lining himself up not so much with the forces of
reaction as with what is permanent in our lives. It is true that the

values of which he approves are represented in the poem by 'old
men in country houses' and not by the old men on their estates but,
for Betjeman, the old king's death is a symbol of the end of an era
from which the whole brash modern world with its garish suburbs
represents a definite falling-off. He is not defending privilege so
much as regretting the departure of an ordered world in which
questions and their answers were clearcut and unswerving as Philip
Larkin was to do in connection with a different, and more
significant, turning-point in his poem 'MCMXIV'.

Nostalgia for a vanished age of certainty is a recurrent theme in
Betjeman's poetry. Nor is it associated only with the passing of
kings: 'Croydon', from *Mount Zion*, laments just as plangently the
death of an obscure individual. Like the other poem, it mourns not
only one man's death but the loss of innocence and security; qualities
which are at a premium in the twentieth century:

> In a house like that
>   Your Uncle Dick was born;
> Satchel on back he walked to Whitgift
>   Every weekday morn.
>
> Boys together in Coulsdon woodlands,
>   Bramble-berried and steep,
> He and his pals would look for spadgers
>   Hidden deep.
>
> The laurels are speckled in Marchmont Avenue
>   Just as they were before,
> But the steps are dusty that still lead up to
>   Your Uncle Dick's front door.
>
> Pear and apple in Croydon gardens
>   Bud and blossom and fall,
> But your Uncle Dick has left his Croydon
>   Once for all.

The statement here is so simple and direct as to require no comment,
save to remark how the characteristic fixing of the scene in a
particular place – 'Boys together in Coulsdon woodlands', 'The
laurels are speckled in Marchmont Avenue' – adds depth and weight
to the emotion, particularizing and placing it, giving both authority
and authenticity to the poet's utterance. The poem recalls a real

person in a real place; it is not simply a facile piece of mock-Victorian sentimentalizing, as a superficial reading might suggest.

The same 'spirit of place' hovers over a better poem, 'Love in a Valley', which first appeared in *Continual Dew*. Its metre and title derive from Meredith, though the mood is subtly different:

> Far, far below me roll the Coulsdon woodlands,
>> White down the valley curves the living rail,
> Tall, tall, above me, olive spike the pinewoods,
>> Olive against blue black, moving in the gale.

The now familiar suburban setting is evoked lovingly:

> Deep down the drive go the cushioned rhododendrons,
>> Deep down, sand deep, drives the heather root,
> Deep the spliced timber barked around the summer-house,
>> Light lies the tennis-court, plantain underfoot.

The comfortable trappings of prosperous suburbia – rustic summer-house, tennis-court, 'metal lantern and white enamelled door', 'the spread of orange from the gas-fire on the carpet', the leaded windows 'lozenging the crimson' – where even the rhododendrons are 'cushioned', are not brought in to mock or belittle the girl who, looking down at the railway lines in the valley, thinks of her absent lover, the Lieutenant:

> Portable Lieutenant! they carry you to China
>> And me to lonely shopping in a brilliant arcade;
> Firm hand, fond hand switch the giddy engine!
>> So for us a last time is bright light made.

Though the mood is light-hearted and tinged with irony and even farce in the cry of agony, 'Portable Lieutenant!', the emotion is none the less genuine; some things manage to be both sad and funny at the same time. It is the things which are easiest to make fun of in this suburban girl – her naïve fondness for the Lieutenant's 'rakish car', the cosy dullness of her life – which serve to sharpen our apprehension of her sadness. Betjeman may regard the 'brilliant arcade' as a tawdry product of bourgeois philistinism but he never denies the humanity of those people of whose lives it is part. While the reference to Meredith is ironical and intended to point a contrast, it would be a mistake to read the poem as satire. His borrowing from Meredith is as much a sign of his fondness for playing about with metre for its own sake, as well as a kind of back-handed tribute to one of his beloved Victorians, as it is a vehicle for satire. Betjeman is certainly not being patronizing or 'clever' in this poem; the emotion is sincere and unaffected though the conscious irony of tone together with the inescapable and freely acknowledged element of parody create a suspicion that it may not be. This ambiguity of response was typical of Betjeman at this time and helps explain the partial misunderstanding of his intentions which afflicted some critics. Satire, it would be safe to say, was rarely his intention. He is simply too fond of his fellow human beings; with the result that even in 'Slough', which begins with a series of savage exhortations whose ferocious savagery might have set Swift reeling –

> Come, friendly bombs, and fall on Slough
> It isn't fit for humans now,
> There isn't grass to graze a cow
>> Swarm over, Death!

— he finds himself pardoning 'the bald young clerks' who add their masters' profits, because they have no choice. He knows they are helpless victims of a depraved system of values:

> It's not their fault they do not know
> The birdsong from the radio,
> It's not their fault they often go
>> To Maidenhead
>
> And talk of sports and makes of cars
> In various bogus Tudor bars
> And daren't look up and see the stars
>> But belch instead.

Towards the vulgar profiteer for whom the young clerks work, however, he is uncharacteristically merciless, invoking the bombs to fall on him, in particular:

> And get that man with double chin
> Who'll always cheat and always win,
> Who washes his repulsive skin
>> In women's tears,

> And smash his desk of polished oak,
> And smash his hands so used to stroke
> And stop his boring dirty joke
>   And make him yell.

For almost the only time, Betjeman here recalls one of his own contemporaries: C. Day Lewis, whose almost contemporary collection, *The Magnetic Mountain*, contains a poem in which he bullies and hectors his own particular *bêtes noires*, the right-wing press barons, in similarly violent terms:

> Scavenger barons and your jackal vassals,
> Your pimping press-gang, your unclean vessels
> We'll make you swallow your words at a gulp
> And turn you back to your element pulp.

It is not as good a poem as Betjeman's and does not contain any redeeming hint of compassion to save it from total hysteria: for Day Lewis, the rich man's underlings share in his guilt and must, therefore, share his fate. Like Betjeman's, only more so, it only succeeds in arousing our sympathy for victims whose gleefully imagined fate seems disproportionate to their offence.

Human mortality, though rarely in this homicidal form, has been a recurrent theme in Betjeman's work. It is the subject of such early poems as 'Exeter' and 'Death in Leamington' – which John Sparrow described as Betjeman's 'Innisfree' 'doomed to haunt him its author, in too persistent popularity, all his days'. Unlike Yeats's, however, Betjeman's poetry has undergone no radical transformation, with the result that 'Death in Leamington', though it has been surpassed, remains a characteristic piece. Despite its familiarity it still has a delectable freshness and sparkle. Its originality lies in the piquant combination of jaunty rhythm and sombre mood so that, as in 'Love in a Valley', there is a slight sense of ambiguity. As always with Betjeman, the place is as important as what happens or the emotions to which it gives rise. In Betjeman, to paraphrase Philip Larkin, something – or, indeed, nothing – happens not *anywhere* but, most definitely, *somewhere*. Place, action and feelings are a unity so that the physical decay of the spa town images the old lady's lingering death:

> Do you know that the stucco is peeling?
> Do you know that the heart will stop?

From those yellow Italianate arches
Do you hear the plaster drop?

The other poem, 'Exeter', is about sudden death, violently and unexpectedly met. While in the earlier poem the death is treated coolly, the poet's attitude being at one with the nurse's clinical matter-of-factness, in 'Exeter' what is undeniably tragic is overlaid with farce. Because of the poet's total detachment, once again we are unsure whether to laugh or to cry. Again, too, the setting is important; among other things, it is a poem about a place. A doctor's bluestocking wife sits in her garden reading a novel by Aldous Huxley. As she turns Huxley's rationalist pages, she is deaf to the cathedral bells which once summoned her to worship:

Once those bells, those Exeter bells
  Called her to praise and pray
By pink, acacia-shaded walls
  Several times a day
To Wulfric's altar and riddel posts
  While the choir sang Stanford in A.

In the next stanza her husband, one of Betjeman's impatient motorists who so frequently come to grief, meets his untimely death:

Clash and whirr down Colleton Crescent,
  Other cars all go hang
My little bus is enough for us –
  Till a tram-car bell went clang.

In the presence of her husband's 'smiling corpse', his intellectual wife no longer finds comfort in Aldous Huxley and the discarded religious faith returns to fill the vacuum:

Now those bells, those Exeter bells
  Call her to praise and pray
By pink, acacia-shaded walls
  Several times a day
To Wulfric's altar and riddel posts
  And the choir sings Stanford in A.

'Exeter' is not one of Betjeman's best poems and the deliberately neutral tone means that both the doctor's death and his wife's response to it fail to convince above the level of mere burlesque. The neat inversion of the two stanzas describing the wife's alternate loss and recovery of her faith is too slick, a device which enables the poet to tie up the ends of his poem neatly. It is, in fact, just a skilful piece of versifying and the pleasure it gives is of the shallow sort afforded by light verse.

The moral neutrality which marks such a poem is also noticeable in 'The Arrest of Oscar Wilde at the Cadogan Hotel'. John Press considers that Betjeman here deliberately plays up 'the absurd elements in the scene in order to conceal his own response to the tragedy of Wilde's downfall'. But the ironic tone seems more appropriate when applied to Oscar Wilde, a rather comic figure, than when applied to deaths of private individuals. The mock-serious ballad form suits the subject perfectly and does more than serve to hide Betjeman's own feelings. Similarly, the 'old stage properties' which John Sparrow feels are wheeled 'all too con-scientiously into place' – the hock and seltzer, and astrakhan coat, the *Yellow Book* – occur only in Wilde's conversation. Like the weak Wildean epigram, 'Approval of what is approved of is as false as a well-kept vow', they serve only to emphasize the absurdity which was an undeniable aspect of Wilde's character; there is no feeling that Betjeman is cynically manipulating stock properties. Betjeman's own evocation of period atmosphere is, in fact, sharp and original:

> To the right and before him Pont Street
>   Did tower in her new built red,
> As hard as the morning gaslight
>   That shone on his unmade bed

There is no stale whiff of the property basket about this; nor does it deny the element of sordid tragedy in Wilde's ignominious end. Certainly, the arrest, with the eruption into capital letters coinciding with the abrupt entry of TWO PLAIN CLOTHES POLICEMEN, is pure farce, but the final stanza is direct and moving:

> He rose, and he put down *The Yellow Book*.
>   He staggered – and, terrible-eyed,
> He brushed past the palms on the staircase
>   And was helped to a hansom outside.

Betjeman does not seem to be concealing anything here; nor are the palms just period properties; they serve to pinpoint the emotion, acting as reminders of the physical world which Wilde is leaving. It remains one of Betjeman's most attractive poems.

Two other linked poems from these years show that Betjeman was no mere eccentric trifler, but a potentially important poet. 'Dorset', the slighter of the two poems, deals, characteristically, with a topographical theme. It is inspired by Hardy's 'Friends Beyond', the poem in which Hardy imagines departed local 'hearts and heads' whispering to him in Mellstock churchyard. For William Dewy, Tranter Reuben, Farmer Ledlow late at plough and the rest, Betjeman substitutes the names of contemporary worthies:

> While Tranter Reuben, T. S. Eliot, H. G. Wells and Edith
> Sitwell lie in Mellstock Churchyard now.

The poem is an entertaining *jeu d'esprit* and a mock-serious footnote explains impishly that 'the names in the last lines of these stanzas are put in not out of malice or satire but merely for their euphony'. He might more truthfully have said that they were put there to amuse his friends.

> While Tranter Reuben, Mary Borden, Brian Howard and
> Harold Acton lie in Mellstock Churchyard now.

Brian Howard and Harold Acton were certainly friends and little known outside a fairly exclusive circle at the time. Indeed, there is a rather disconcerting suggestion of the private joke about the poem, both in the choice of names and in the coy footnote. Such in-jokes were not uncommon in the thirties and the work of Auden and his friends are packed with such private references. But whilst Betjeman may have written such poems to amuse a select private audience, they have lasted well, proving that he was something more than court jester to the smart set.

As well as being in part, a private joke, 'Dorset' is also a tribute to Hardy and the Dorset landscape. 'Mellstock' in Hardy's poem is the village of Stinsford where his heart is buried, a fact which forms the basis of the other poem – written at the same time though, inexplicably, not published in book form until 1958 – 'The Heart of Thomas Hardy'. Philip Larkin has called it 'totally eccentric' though, in fact, it is less impenetrable than some of Betjeman's other poems. Nevertheless, it contains some rather odd conceits. Hardy's heart, likened to 'a little thumping fig' as it shoots over the elms in the churchyard, flies to God, who waits in a golden nimbus, whereupon a bizarre apotheosis of Hardy's fictional characters is enacted:

Slowly out of the grass, slitting the mounds in the centre
Riving apart the roots, rose the new covered corpses
Tess and Jude and His Worship, various unmarried mothers,
Woodmen, cutters of turf, adulterers, church restorers,
Turning aside the stones thump on the upturned churchyard.
Soaring over the elm trees slower than Thomas Hardy,
Weighted down with a Conscience, now for the first time
                                                 fleshly
Taking form as a growth hung from the feet like a sponge-bag.

The image of conscience as a sponge-bag-like growth depending from the feet of a new-risen corpse is strange as, indeed, is that of the poet's heart 'twittering' in the divine effulgence. It suggests, if anything, the sort of images to be found in Roman Catholic devotional pictures of the more lurid kind; though Donald Davie goes a little too far when he calls it 'Dantesque'. Nevertheless, the poem is an impressive achievement and, in its skilful mastery of a difficult metrical scheme, it shows what an accomplished craftsman Betjeman was even at this early stage.

Though Betjeman, according to his reviewers, was already something more than just 'a satirist of bourgeois civilization' (Tom Driberg); 'a passionate observer of the second-rate' (Peter Quennell); or a poet whose 'poetry is not meant to be read but recited – and recited with almost epileptic animation' (Evelyn Waugh), it would be a mistake to ignore any of these aspects of his early, or indeed later, work. One must guard against being over-solemn when discussing the work of this poet: the last laugh may well be on the commentator. In fact, with the exception of those poems already discussed, the other poems in these two early collections resolve themselves into three discrete groups: satirical (for example, 'The City'); knockabout farce ('The 'Varsity Students' Rag'); and, by far the largest group, comic digressions on the various party divisions within the Church of England as well as explorations of the dimmer reaches of non-conformity ('Hymn'; 'Competition').

As satire, 'Slough' fails because of its intemperate and quite uncharacteristic savagery: a sledge-hammer seems to have been used to crack a walnut. Despite its manifest faults, however, 'Slough' stays in the mind; its very ferocity ensures that it gets a hearing. The other satires in these early collections are, alas, all too forgettable. 'Camberley', for instance, is both slight and tiresomely snobbish. Its delineation of gruesome suburban tribal rites may have given its early audience a delicious *frisson*, but the poem leads nowhere. The target, such as it is, is suburban respectability, affectionately parodied rather than subjected to withering scorn. 'Knock gently', the insidiously 'refained' voice suggests,

> don't disturb the maid,
> She's got to clear, and I'm afraid
> That she is less inclined to take
> The blame than Mrs Kittiwake.

What the reader is meant to infer from this is presumably that servants are getting a bit above themselves these days, precisely the sort of complaint which the genteelly poor Kittiwakes might be expected to make. But what, we wonder, is the maid unwilling to take the blame for? One feels that Betjeman was simply looking for a rhyme and that the whole poem was dashed off quickly, a product of Betjeman's fatal facility.

'The City' has an equally extemporary quality about it, appearing to have been abandoned before it really got started. It begins by tilting at a familiar target: the rich, ugly, lustful capitalist. The 'Business men with awkward hips /And dirty jokes upon their lips' are coevals of the man 'Who'll always cheat and always win' in 'Slough'. The poem, however, is left suspended in mid-air; its final couplet –

> But father, son and clerk join up
> To talk about the Football Cup

– seeming contrived and irrelevant, a brave and sudden climax to an impromptu performance. One is left with a fragment, an off-the-cuff vignette rather than a finished poem, but one which Betjeman was too pleased with simply to throw away.

Two suburban satires from these years have not been reprinted in the *Collected Poems*. One of them, 'The Other Suburbs', is a patronizing look at suburban gentility: bright kitchenettes, stained-glass windows, 'Drage-way drawing-room' where 'wifie knits through hubbie's gloom'. The observation is characteristically acute but what is particularly displeasing about this sort of poem – as, indeed, about a later and more familiar piece, 'How to Get On in Society' – is the way in which Betjeman mocks one form of snobbery from the standpoint of another; the petty snobberies of the suburbs from the grander ones of the country house.

'The Garden City', with its parodic echo of T. E. Brown's famous lyric, 'A garden is a lovesome thing, God wot!', is rather better.

> O wot ye why in Orchard Way
> The roofs be steep and shelving?
> Or wot ye what the dwellers say
> In close and garden delving?

The poem pokes gentle fun at the cosy *folklorique* pretensions of the Ruskin- and Morris-inspired suburban arts and crafts movement which had produced the garden cities of Letchworth and Welwyn and, more prettily, Hampstead Garden Suburb:

> 'Hand-woven be my wefts, hand-made
>   My pottery for pottage,
> And hoe and mattock, aye, and spade,
>   Hang up about my cottage.'

Despite the tone of sophisticated condescension in these poems, they are neither savage nor indignant. Betjeman, it is plain, is rather fond of the suburbs, despite their comical pretensions. Affection and curiosity are more apparent than hate. The security of the lives lived in suburban homesteads makes a strong emotional appeal to him and he is intrigued rather than outraged by the perversities of suburban taste. While he abhors the makeshift appearance of Slough with its dedication to the twentieth-century gods of profit and loss, he is conscious of the pathos of its less fortunate inhabitants, forced to live in a hell which is not of their own making. Similarly, he finds much which is appealing in lush and well-established suburbs such as Camberley which, for all their smugness, are genuinely expressive of human needs.

One of the performance poems from *Mount Zion* which has stood up relatively well is 'The 'Varsity Students' Rag', a boisterous lampoon on the subject of college hearties ('You want to have the 'varsity touch after a public school'). It was intended for the kind of manic declamation which characterized Betjeman's own impromptu recitals of 'D'ye ken Kolkhorst?' at Oxford. It is a spirited piece which still goes with a swing despite its decidedly period flavour. It was obviously written for a specific audience as were those contemporary Oxford pieces which mock the dim, serious-minded sort of undergraduate: as much objects of the hedonistic and frivolous Betjeman's scorn as the back-slapping hearties whose idea of fun was smashing 'rotten old pictures which were priceless works of art'. In 'Tea with the Poets', from *Continual Dew*,

> Three pink Hampstead intellectuals,
> Three thin *passé* Bloomsbury dons
> Sit discussing Manley Hopkins
> Over Mr Grogley's dainty scones.

It is the sort of gathering at which the productions of the Left Book Club would be read and the poems of the 'pylon poets' admired. In fact, mention is made of two of these: 'friends of Stephen Spender lie at ease' and 'C. Day Lewis brings his wolf cubs'. His own friends, Auden and MacNeice, who were the other constituents of 'Macspaunday' – Roy Campbell's collective term for them – are not mentioned, however. Betjeman, then as now, was nothing if not loyal.

The subject of the three other Oxford poems – 'A Hike on the Downs', 'The Wykehamist' and 'The Wykehamist at Home' – has been identified as the late Richard Crossman, an intimate acquaintance of Auden's but not until much later a friend of Betjeman's. In 'A Hike on the Downs', a Platonist don – Crossman published *Plato Today* in 1937 – takes his young protégé on a walking tour round Winchester:

> 'You take your pipe – that will impress
>   Your strength on anyone who passes;
> I'll take my *Plautus (non purgatus)*
>   And both my pairs of horn-rimmed glasses.'

The poem is rather uninspired, falling back on such references as the almost obligatory one to C. S. Lewis ('do you think he's *quite* first rate?'), which only the initiated were expected to understand. Like 'The City' and 'Camberley', it gives the impression of being not quite finished, a little treat served up for the delectation of an admiring circle of personal friends.

'The Wykehamist', however, is both funny and extremely accomplished. It shows Betjeman at his most impish and delightful. It

is dedicated to Randolph Churchill with the assurance that it is
'not about him', though there is nothing hermetic about its references.

> 'Tis not for us to wonder why
> He wears that curious knitted tie;
> We should not cast reflections on
> The very slightest kind of don.
> We should not giggle as we like
> At his appearance on his bike;
> It's something to become a bore,
> And more than that, at twenty-four.

Its companion piece, 'The Wykehamist at Home', is one of the
poems which Betjeman has chosen not to reprint. While it is a good
deal less brilliant than its predecessor, it reveals Betjeman's attitude
towards those do-gooders whose motives for befriending working-
class youths were not always entirely disinterested. The words
which he puts into the Wykehamist's mouth are clear enough:

> 'Jolly old Winchester! Jolly old New College!
>   Cream of our fine middle classes!
> By cheerful unbendings in soccer and social clubs
>   *We* can get on with the masses.'

By far the largest group of poems in these two early collections
springs from Betjeman's passionate interest in the varieties of
worship within the Anglican communion, the differences – both
social and doctrinal – between 'High' and 'Low' and 'Broad' and
from his fascination with chapels and meeting-houses of obscure
non-conformist sects. By no stretch of the imagination could these
be called religious or devotional poems. Almost always, the intention is to amuse; though the seriousness of Betjeman's interest in
the subject is obvious. No one who did not love the church could
have written the rollicking 'Our Padre', which is about one of those
hearty Broad-Churchmen who are not much to Betjeman's taste;
any more than someone who did not love the suburbs could have
written 'The Garden City' or 'Love in a Valley'.

As well as poems which look wryly at the Church of England,
there are some strange and grim pieces – 'For Nineteenth-Century
Burials' and 'Calvinistic Evensong' – which reveal the darker side
of Betjeman's nature. In the first of these, he writes of the physical

horror of death with the kind of rapt fascination which characterizes many of his later poems:

> The gentle fingers are touching to pray
> Which crumple and straighten for Death.

In 'Calvinistic Evensong' a chilling vision of the intolerance and joylessness of this uncompromising faith is conjured up:

> For Calvin now the soft oil lamps are lit
> Hands on their hymnals six old women sit.
> Black gowned and sinister, he now appears
> Curate-in-charge of aged parish fears.
> Let, unaccompanied, that psalm begin
> Which deals most harshly with the fruits of sin!

Such a religion, which depends on fear and in which only 'the chosen saints here below' are guaranteed salvation, is deeply repugnant to Betjeman, especially in its denial of pleasure and its repudiation of even the most trivial kind of vanity. It seems to him not only cruel but ultimately life-denying:

> And that mauve hat three cherries decorate
> Next week shall topple from its trembling perch
> While wet fields reek like some long empty church.

Another poem combines this sense of horror with a sense of farce. 'Suicide on Junction Road Station after Abstention from Evening Communion in North London' is, despite its sombre subject, essentially a light-hearted piece as its long title, which serves to guy the subject, obviously suggests. The opening stanza with its reference to the gas mantle, so characteristic a feature of Low-Church worship, and the ardent evangelical's identification of his own spiritual ecstasy with its roar, sets the tone:

> With the roar of the gas my heart gives a shout –
> To Jehovah Tsidkenu the praise!
> Bracket and bracket go blazon it out
> In this Evangelical haze!

'Undenominational', too, affectionately mocks the 'enthusiasm' of the evangelicals whose souls are saved in overheated conventicles:

Revival ran along the hedge
And made my spirit whole
When steam was on the window panes
And glory in my soul.

In 'Distant View of a Provincial Town' – believed to be Reading
– Betjeman turns his attention to the Church of England. He sees
from his railway carriage the various churches and reflects on the
different kinds of worship being carried on within them: 'High' St
Aidan's, 'Low' St George's, 'Broad' St Mary's and, finally, the
neglected United Benefice which looks even more sad 'since Mr
Grogley' – familiar from 'Tea with the Poets' – 'was unfrocked'.
Though the poem is gaily satirical and irreverent, it concludes on a
serious note, and so reveals the solemn core at the heart of Betjeman's
high spirits:

The old Great Western Railway shakes
The old Great Western Railway spins –
The old Great Western Railway makes
Me very sorry for my sins.

While in 'Exchange of Livings' he pokes gentle fun at the Church
of England, in a more spirited and accomplished piece, 'Competition', unaccountably missing from succeeding editions of *Collected
Poems*, he records the bitter rivalry, as ferocious as that between
rival supermarkets, which broke out among the various non-
conformist sects during the nineteenth century. The inducements
which were on offer were far from spiritual:

The Gothic is bursting over the way
With Evangelical Song,
For the pinnacled Wesley Memorial Church
Is over a hundred strong,
And what is a new Jerusalem
Gas-lit and yellow wall'd
To a semi-circular pitch-pine sea
With electric light install'd?

The poem is brought off with tremendous panache and wit and
demonstrates Betjeman's ability to penetrate the past imaginatively
and bring it alive. For Betjeman, the passions involved in this
absurd competition for the cure of souls seemed more real and far

more comprehensible than the contemporary political events which were obsessing most of his fellow poets. The great events of the time – the rise of Fascism, mass unemployment, the Spanish Civil War – passed Betjeman by because his attention was engaged elsewhere.

In 'Hymn', a conscious parody of 'The Church's One Foundation', he turns his attention towards the Victorian church restorers who wreaked such havoc on the fabric of medieval buildings with their passion for improvement. Although he admires Victorian architecture in its pure form, he is pained by those acts of vandalism in which old box pews were ripped out to make way for varnished pitch-pine and the mellow tones of age replaced with the garish hues of cheap stained glass, burnished brass and violently coloured tiles. These tasteless and vulgar works of restoration typified the adamantine self-confidence of the Victorians, who genuinely believed that their work was sanctioned by God. By adopting the rhythms of the hymn book, Betjeman mischievously exposes and ridicules this unbecoming state of mind. It is, without doubt, the best of these poems in which Betjeman plays about with ecclesiastical themes.

> O worthy persecution
>   Of dust! O hue divine!
> O cheerful substitution,
>   Thou varnishéd pitch-pine!
>
> Church furnishing! Church furnishing!
>   Sing art and crafty praise!
> He gave the brass for burnishing
>   He gave the thick red baize,
> He gave the new addition,
>   Pull'd down the dull old aisle,
> – To pave the sweet transition
>   He gave th'encaustic tile.

Although Betjeman's interest in congregation and clergy, not to mention architecture, seems to operate almost to the exclusion of divine mysteries, only a deeply religious man would interest himself in such things. His love of God is not open to doubt. He loves the Church as something typically English, as irritating, eccentric and fascinating as the public schools or the suburbs. These early poems, in fulfilment of his father's advice, are both funny and original. They are instinct, however, with serious concern and strong emotion.

Betjeman's friends and admirers of the thirties regarded him as eccentric, someone refreshingly different from his contemporaries. Auden thought of him in much the same way that he thought of P. G. Wodehouse, a consummate craftsman and a superb entertainer. But Betjeman was something more than an entertainer or a sophisticated parodist wryly setting up echoes of Victorian writers for the amusement of the *cognoscenti* and mocking Englishry with schoolboy delight. Beneath the surface irony and technical polish, there was deep seriousness. His passion for neglected and drab settings – suburbs, Victorian railways, decaying spas, non-conformist chapels – was evidence of an original mind and this highly personal vision was pursued with profound conviction. His poems represented something more than a self-conscious assumption of eccentricity, a wilful flight from the poetic orthodoxies of the time. He subscribed to Auden's dictum: 'Report well: begin with objects and events'; though he was more than a reporter. From the start, he was an entirely serious artist; his seriousness has simply become more apparent over the years.

CHAPTER THREE

TOPOPHILIA

Although both the early collections had been praised by a fairly small circle of devoted admirers, they had not succeeded in establishing Betjeman as anything more than a minority taste. The next two collections – *Old Lights for New Chancels* (1940) and *New Bats in Old Belfries* (1945) – eschewed the typographical eccentricities and decorative flourishes of the earlier volumes which, in retrospect, seemed suspiciously like camouflage designed to conceal what was essentially a very minor talent. In contrast, these two wartime collections, doubtless as a result of wartime austerity standards, were plain, even drab, little books. The poems they contain, however, are considerably better: less cautiously ironic, more obviously serious.

Old Lights for New Chancels is prefaced by a short note in which Betjeman explains his themes and lists some of his influences. It is a sort of apologia, a partial attempt to clear up some of the misunderstandings which had already begun to cluster round his work and which were making it difficult for him to be taken seriously. He was aware of the danger that his genuine passion for suburbs and chapels and railways would be dismissed as a comic turn or a sophisticated pose. His admirers, while capable of appreciating the poems he wrote about such things, were incapable of sharing, or even understanding, the strength of his emotional attachment to them.

In his prefatory note, he explains that he is moved to write poems because of his 'topographical predilection': in particular, by his fondness for 'suburbs and gaslights and Pont Street and Gothic

Revival churches and mineral railways, provincial towns and garden cities'. He is at pains to point out that when he is writing about the suburbs he is 'not being satirical but topographical'. He goes on to say that he admires poets like Crabbe, Burns, Tennyson, William Barnes, Hood and Praed 'not for their finer flights, but for their topographical atmosphere'. He says he also finds this same atmosphere in the works of less celebrated writers than these: 'I can find great pleasure in what is termed minor poetry, in long epics which never get into anthologies; topographical descriptions in verse published locally.'

In 1944, Betjeman brought out an anthology with his friend Geoffrey Taylor: *English, Scottish and Welsh Landscape*, which was illustrated by John Piper. It was an attempt to rehabilitate and lift out of obscurity the writings of some of these 'quiet Georgian rectors, village schoolmasters, peers in their libraries looking across the park, Victorian drunks and reformers and escapists' who observed the landscape about them and recorded their impressions in verse. In its patient recording of visual details their work resembled topographical painting rather than the lyrical outpourings of the great poets of nature. Wordsworth gazed at nature in a mood of philosophical rapture rather than as a quiet recorder of what he saw; there was, for him, a sort of morality in the natural world. Betjeman, like the minor poets he admires, is content to observe and record; he uncovers no metaphysical truths.

The ideas expressed in the preface to *Old Lights for New Chancels* were picked up by John Sparrow in the introduction which he wrote for *Selected Poems* (1948). He described Betjeman as 'a painter of the particular, the recognizable, landscape' though he differed from other such poets in not being restricted to one specific locality. Unlike Crabbe in Suffolk, Cowper in Buckinghamshire and Barnes in Dorset, Betjeman is 'equally at home in the most diverse surroundings'. In these two collections there are, in fact, poems about Berkshire, the Midlands, Ireland, East Anglia, Cornwall, London, Oxford, the Thames Valley and Surrey, each of which is observed with equal fidelity. Furthermore, as Sparrow also observed, he was not just interested in landscape *qua* landscape but in the people for whose lives it forms a background. Auden, too, spoke of this 'topographical predilection' of Betjeman's in the admiring introduction he wrote for his American selection from Betjeman's poetry and prose, coining the word 'topophilia' to describe it.

When one looks at the very early poems – with the exception of 'Love in a Valley' in which the well-furnished Surrey landscape is observed closely – there is an absence of precise description. 'Camberley' contains stock references to 'Surrey pines' and the 'Surrey dark', just as 'Exeter' mentions 'those Exeter bells', without saying how they differ from pines (or bells) elsewhere. In 'Dorset' the county is evoked simply by listing the names, albeit suggestive, of some of its villages:

Rime Intrinsica, Fontmell Magna, Sturminster Newton and
          Melbury Bubb,
Whist upon whist upon whist upon whist drive in Institute,
         Legion and Social Club.

Indeed, the same could be said of 'Cheltenham', the first poem in *Old Lights for New Chancels* which – apart from a reference to 'the stuccoed afternoon' which would have served equally well in 'Death in Leamington' – contains no actual description at all.

This is not to say, of course, that these poems fail on that account. Betjeman's 'topographical predilection' extends beyond appearance to what happens in a particular place; he responds to what is characteristic or typical of a place as well as to what it looks like. However, these two wartime collections show Betjeman beginning to produce poems which lyrically evoke landscape in a way that is very different from the mood of the earlier poems. The impulse in 'Exeter' or 'Camberley' is primarily satiric (at least, comic) rather than the desire to preserve a memory of a particular place at a particular time. Betjeman focuses on the human inhabitants – the retired Anglo-Indian couple in 'Camberley', the doctor's intellectual wife in 'Exeter' – and the topographical setting is incidental though expressive. In the later and more mature poems, this situation is reversed so that, in John Sparrow's words, 'the figures in the foreground . . . are subordinate to their setting'. The backdrop has become more important than the play.

Topographical poems form the bulk of these two wartime collections and their mood is as varied as their setting. 'A Shropshire Lad', though its title suggests Housman's doom-laden young farm labourers, is about the Channel swimmer, Captain Webb, who, a note informs the reader, 'was born at Dawley in an industrial district in Salop'. John Press has neatly described the poem as 'a mock-serious ghost story which moves to one of Betjeman's most captivating tunes'. Betjeman's note tells us that the poem 'should be recited with a Midland accent' and the poet himself has given a memorable performance to a musical accompaniment, redolent of brass bands, composed by Mr Jim Parker. It is essentially a comic piece but also rather more than that. There is a delightful ambiguity about it which makes it more typical of the poems in *Continual Dew* than what was to come later. Although the non-conformist industrial setting is fondly described, there is more than a touch of irony in the sham-solemn footnote which explains that the first line was suggested by *Boyhood*, 'A novel in verse by Rev. E. E. Bradford, D.D.'

> The gas was on in the Institute,
>   The flare was up in the gym,
> A man was running a mineral line,
>   A lass was singing a hymn.
> When Captain Webb the Dawley man,
>   Captain Webb from Dawley,
> Came swimming along the old canal
>   That carried the bricks to Lawley.

The poem continues in this vein. Webb's thrifty, non-conformist ghost finds time for practical and terrestrial concerns as it swims along to its destination ('And paying a call at Dawley Bank while swimming along to Heaven'). Having settled its finances, it continues its watery anabasis until, to their amazement, the prosaic congregation see

> Webb in a water sheeting,
> Come dripping along in a bathing dress
>   To the Saturday evening meeting.
>   Dripping along –
>   Dripping along –
>   To the Congregational Hall;
> Dripping and still he rose over the sill
>   and faded away in a wall.

Such a poem raises the question of how seriously Betjeman could really be taken after all. To the more sophisticated section of his audience it must have seemed that he was being merely ironical, that the allusion to the Reverend Bradford (who?) and the absurd tragi-comic subject were intended merely to mock provincial mediocrity and dimness. But Betjeman, we remember, loves 'mineral railways [and] provincial towns'; he also loves neglected nineteenth-century poems, such as those by the Reverend Bradford, 'which never get into anthologies'. The ironical edge is, to some extent, supplied by the reader albeit with the poet's connivance. It should be remembered that Betjeman is not merely being clever or setting out simply to amuse us. Provincial dimness, though it amuses him as well, moves him more than metropolitan brightness. He is, nevertheless, well aware that from the standpoint of metro-politan sophistication, what he writes about Captain Webb must appear to be tinged with irony. It is part of the complex double-bluff which characterizes so much of his work: saying something which one feels sincerely in such a way that it appears insincere or, at least, mildly facetious, and relishing the apparent perversity.

His uniqueness among modern poets is partially accounted for by an eccentric sensibility which is genuinely and profoundly moved by things outside the range and understanding of the more intelligent and sophisticated section of his audience, but which is, at the same time, sufficiently self-aware to take their likely response into account and consciously play upon it. He is both self-conscious and completely genuine, a highly original combination. Without the self-conscious irony, a poem such as 'A Shropshire Lad' would seem trite and sentimental; without the genuine emotion underpin-ning its irony, it would seem merely clever.

'Upper Lambourne', about the Berkshire village famed for its racing stables, is, by contrast, straightforwardly elegiac and lyrical. It is an example of Betjeman's keen observation and his intensely personal response to landscape and its human associations. The poet's eye seems to move in like a camera lens, as it seeks out the grave which is the emotional nexus of the poem:

> Up the ash-tree climbs the ivy,
>   Up the ivy climbs the sun,
> With a twenty-thousand pattering
>   Has a valley breeze begun,
> Feathery ash, neglected elder,
>   Shift the shade and make it run –
>
> Shift the shade toward the nettles,
>   And the nettles set it free
> To streak the stained Carrara headstone
>   Where, in nineteen-twenty-three,

> He who trained a hundred winners
> Paid the Final Entrance Fee.

Though on first reading the last line might seem to strike a jarring, facetious note, on subsequent readings its suggestion of a down-to-earth acceptance of death, a readiness almost to make a joke of it, seems entirely appropriate for a racehorse trainer who might be expected to have little time for conventional pieties.

From the close-up of the gravestone, the camera moves over to the 'spreading stables' and finally pans out to take in the whole majestic sweep of the Berkshire countryside. At this point, the verse assumes a suitably solemn and valedictory note which has both amplitude and richness, like a slow movement by Elgar:

> Feathery ash in leathery Lambourne
> Waves above the sarsen stone,
> And Edwardian plantations
> So coniferously moan
> As to make the swelling downland,
> Far-surrounding, seem their own.

The landscape of 'Upper Lambourne' is unpeopled. It is a landscape of mood, its natural features consciously arranged by the poet, like notes in music, to evoke a particular state of feeling. Thus, we note that the elders, like the grave, are 'neglected'; that the string of horses, like their dead trainers, are 'moving out of sight and mind'; that the pine plantations, as if in mourning for the man who once lived among them, 'coniferously moan'. It is all brought off very decorously but there is also a certain stiltedness about it. It is less a spontaneous response to a particular place than a conscious exercise in arrangement; the opening stanzas can be read almost as stage directions, telling the landscape how to comport itself.

Betjeman is happier with a landscape in which he can respond to living human associations. For all its formal beauty and lyrical grace, 'Upper Lambourne' is less impressive than the more robust and virile 'Henley-on-Thames'. If 'Upper Lambourne' might be likened to an easel painting, highly finished and glowing mellowly through obscuring layers of varnish, 'Henley-on-Thames' is a quick sketch, vivid and sparkling:

When shall I see the Thames again?
The prow-promoted gems again,
  As beefy ATS
  Without their hats
Come shooting through the bridge?

As John Press says, the poem 'is saved from sinking into an inertly sentimental reverie by the solidity of the two stalwart young women'. In this poem, the human inhabitants are, quite literally, the spirit of the place. While the poet might wonder when he will see the Thames again, his poem is a celebration of life rather than an elegy. Betjeman is making a rapturous affirmation rather than indulging a mood of nostalgic regret.

In mud and elder-scented shade
A reach away the breach is made
  By dive and shout
  That circles out
To Henley tower and town;
  And 'Boats for Hire' the rafters ring,
  And pink on white the roses cling,
  And red the bright geraniums swing
In baskets dangling down.

'Ireland with Emily' is Betjeman's most beautiful tribute to the Irish landscape and its people who, at the time he wrote it, seemed still to live in an age of faith, uncorrupted by consumerism and the shallow sophistication it confers. It remains one of his finest poems; the intricate and pleasantly lilting metre is a particular pleasure, form and content achieving a perfect unity:

Bells are booming down the bohreens,
  White the mist along the grass.
Now the Julias, Maeves and Maureens
  Move between the fields to Mass.

It is the neglected aspect of the Irish landscape, its melancholy air of running unconcernedly to seed which appeals to Betjeman.

In yews and woodbine, walls and guelder,
  Nettle-deep the faithful rest,
Winding leagues of flowering elder,
  Sycamore with ivy dressed,

Ruins in demesnes deserted,
Bog-surrounded bramble-skirted –
Townlands rich or townlands mean as
These, oh, counties of them screen us
   In the Kingdom of the West.

Stony seaboard, far and foreign,
   Stony hills poured over space,
Stony outcrop of the Burren,
   Stones in every fertile place,
Little fields with boulders dotted,
Grey-stone shoulders saffron-spotted,
Stone-walled cabins thatched with reeds,
Where a Stone Age people breeds
   The last of Europe's stone age race.

G. S. Fraser considered this last line 'harsh' because it suggested that the native Irish peasantry were primitive savages. Certainly, when contrasted with his approving treatment of the Anglo-Irish ascendancy it may be taken as an example of Betjeman's social snobbery. He has never disguised his love of these aristocratic families and their fine houses and is more regretful at the passing of the world which produced the eighteenth-century streets of Dublin and the glories of Castletown than he is at the sufferings of the oppressed native Irish. 'Ireland with Emily' ends in a spirited tribute to the Anglo-Irish gentry very different from the apparently contemptuous dismissal of the 'Stone Age' peasantry in whose land the desolate mausoleum of one of these great families stands:

There in pinnacled protection,
   One extinguished family waits
A Church of Ireland resurrection
   By the broken, rusty gates.
Sheepswool, straw and droppings cover,
Graves of spinster, rake and lover,
Whose fantastic mausoleum
Sings its own seablown Te Deum,
   In and out the slipping slates.

But, as so often with Betjeman – as, indeed, with many other writers – lack of sympathy with his social attitudes should not blind one to his artistry. In this poem, metrical skill and verbal felicity combine to delightful effect. The Irish landscape in its combined lushness ('Down the bohreens fuchsia-high') and barrenness ('Little fields with boulders dotted') is beautifully evoked. Betjeman has a landscape painter's visual sense combined with a curiosity about the lives carried on in particular settings ('See the black-shawled congregations') and an acute historical imagination ('Ruins in demesnes deserted') which make him a superb topographical poet, one who is responsive to the atmosphere of a place as well as to its appearance. 'Ireland with Emily' remains one of his best poems.

He has written equally well, however, about other landscapes which have personal associations; particularly about the landscapes of his childhood, Cornwall and East Anglia. 'East Anglian Bathe' recalls childhood holidays on the Norfolk Broads while 'Trebetherick', a better poem, recalls holidays in his beloved Cornwall. The poem celebrates the sea in all its varying moods but particularly when it was rough and wild, sending great waves of water 'flooding up the lane' near where their house stood. Above all, however, it is a celebration of the lost world of childhood when waves seemed 'full of treasure' and life, by implication, full of promise. It ends with a prayer that the happiness he experienced in childhood may also be granted to his own children:

> Blessèd be St Enodoc, blessèd be the wave,
> Blessèd be the springy turf, we pray, pray to thee,
> Ask for our children all the happy days you gave
> To Ralph, Vasey, Alastair, Biddy, John and me.

Betjeman has never been afraid of appearing sentimental and a passage such as this could seem mawkish and embarrassing, the sort of sentiment which would not look out of place on a woolwork sampler or some frightful souvenir of Polperro. But Betjeman does not romanticize childhood in this or other poems, despite the rather too fulsome tone of its final invocation. As well as picnics and the excitements of the sea, childhood contains a sense of lurking terror, a feeling that evil is something tangible, lying in wait, biding its time in anticipation of an attack:

> And there the Shade of Evil could
> Stretch out at us from Shilla Mill.
> Thick with sloe and blackberry, uneven in the light,

> Lonely ran the hedge, the heavy meadow was remote,
> The oldest part of Cornwall was the wood as black as night,
> And the pheasant and the rabbit lay torn open at the throat.

The technical mastery shown by Betjeman in his control of the long lines in the poem and his acute apprehension of violence and terror, signalled by the choice of adjectives ('thick', 'uneven', 'lonely', 'heavy') as well as by the dramatic image of the pheasant and the rabbit killed mercilessly and without reason by an unseen, unknown assailant, make 'Trebetherick' a better poem than the trite senti-mentality of its concluding lines, taken out of context, might suggest.

'Parliament Hill Fields', one of Betjeman's best-known poems, is about the part of London in which he grew up.

> Rumbling under blackened girders, Midland, bound for
> Cricklewood,
> Puffed its sulphur to the sunset where that Land of Laundries
> stood.
> Rumble under, thunder over, train and tram alternate go,
> Shake the floor and smudge the ledger, Charrington, Sells,
> Dale & Co.,
> Nuts and nuggets in the window, trucks along the line below.

The comfortable Edwardian world and the particular atmosphere of this part of London are evoked by the precise selection of significant detail – the names of shops and a block of mansion flats, the exact period and style of a named church. The rhythm of the verse suggests the tram's clanging journey, though in the last stanza it subsides into a softer and more contemplative music, achieves a sort of dying fall which succeeds in being Edwardianly moving. The human misery and poverty underlying this lush world of prosperous tradesmen, mansion flats 'flashing fine French-window fire' and tennis on municipal lawns is suggested in the poignant image of children carrying wild flowers home to their slum dwellings in Kentish Town, a sight which moves the pampered middle-class child and awakens compassion, the stranger at the feast in the materialistic world he inhabits.

> Oh the after-tram-ride quiet, when we heard a mile beyond,
> Silver music from the bandstand, barking dogs by Highgate
> Pond;

Up the hill where stucco houses in Virginia creeper drown –
And my childish wave of pity, seeing children carrying down
Sheaves of drooping dandelions to the courts of Kentish Town.

'Parliament Hill Fields' has something of the quality of one of those
old sepia-tinted photographs of London street scenes for which
Betjeman has written captions in a series of topographical books
published by Batsford. It is, however, no mere generalized and
nostalgic vision of the past but a sharply realized picture, firmly
rooted in personal recollection.

Betjeman's response to a place could, nevertheless, be as easily
triggered off by some artefact – an old drawing, for instance, in 'On
an Old-Fashioned Water-Colour of Oxford' – as by actual experience. 'South London Sketch, 1844' has a silver-point delicacy, a
period scent as affecting and artificial as that of a summer rose
pressed between the pages of a Victorian scrapbook. The vanished
rural world which was once London is evoked with as much feeling
and concern for detail as if it were a remembered scene:

> Lavender Sweep is drowned in Wandsworth,
> Drowned in jessamine up to the neck,
> Beetles sway upon bending grass leagues
> Shoulder-level to Tooting Bec.

A similar poem, 'Blackfriars', was suggested by memories of
Wemmick and 'The Agéd' from *Great Expectations*. It conjures up a
vision of Dickensian London, when the dirt of the city was mixed
with the smells of the country, which is also vaguely reminiscent of
T. S. Eliot's 'Preludes'.

> When the sunset in the side streets
> Brought the breezes up the tide,
> Floated bits of daily journals,
> Stable smells and silverside.

Betjeman's unashamed love of the past may appear escapist, a
nostalgic recidivist's obstinate refusal to come to terms with the age
in which he lives on account of its greater complexity and vitality;
a blinkered preference for the easy allurements of personal recollection and historical reverie. But, for Betjeman, the past is complex
and vital, neither a personal haven nor an ivory tower. Just as he is
aware that childhood contains cruelties and disappointments as well

as cosy felicities, he is aware that the past is not merely a picture gallery of comforting images to set against twentieth-century chaos and ugliness. Indeed, when he has written avowedly historical poems, their subject matter has tended to be horrific. One thinks of the parson's fearful adventure in 'A Lincolnshire Tale' or the story of betrayal and ultimate degradation told in the balladic 'Sir John Piers'.

This poem was inspired by a story which Betjeman had discovered in the *Annals of Westmeath, Ancient and Modern*. Piers was a Regency rake, typically 'mad, bad and dangerous to know' who, for a wager, undertook to debauch the wife of his neighbour Lord Cloncurry. His plot was discovered, however, and he was put on trial for criminal conspiracy. His case lost and his fortunes ruined, he fled to the Isle of Man. Eventually, he returned to Ireland and ended his days in a cottage surrounded by a high wall at Tristernagh. It is a spirited and accomplished poem, something of a *tour de force*, with its skilful internal rhymes, its well-managed transitions and subtle variations of mood. It charts the stages of Piers's downfall beginning with the first sighting of Lady Cloncurry at a gay 'Fête Champêtre' followed by 'The Attempt' on her virtue, 'The Exile', 'The Return' and, finally, a description of 'Tristernagh To-day' in which the simple Irish ballad writer, whom Betjeman is impersonating, visits the neglected site and sees a fearful apparition. It is a fine piece of writing, combining horror and farce in much the same way as Robert Graves's 'Welsh Incident'.

> Holy Virgin! What's that emergin'?
> I daren't go down in the place of graves,
> Head of a dragonfly, twenty times magnified,
> Creeping diagonal, out of the caves!
>
> Dockleaves lapping it, maidenhair flapping it,
> Blue veins mapping it, skin of the moon,
> Suck of the bog in it, cold of the frog in it,
> Keep it away from me, shrouded cocoon.
> The worms are moving this soft and smooth thing
> And I'm the creature for foolish fears,
> There's not a feature that's super nature
> 'Tis only rational, 'tis
> SIR
> JOHN
> PIERS.

Less successful than 'Sir John Piers' is another poem inspired by an incident encountered in an old book, 'An Incident in the Early Life of Ebenezer Jones, Poet, 1828'. Jones was one of those minor and now almost forgotten Victorian poets of whom Betjeman is so inordinately fond and whose characteristic manner he consciously assumes in this poem. The incident occurred during Jones's school-days, when he attempted to prevent a cruel schoolmaster from ill-treating a dog which had strayed into the classroom on a very hot summer's day. His brother Sumner Jones's prose account is printed at the head of the poem so that one is reminded of the exercise which his father had set the young Betjeman when they saw Frank Bromley's *The Hopeless Dawn* in the Tate. Betjeman, quite literally, translates the rather pedestrian prose account into verse, extracting every last drop of melodrama from it in the process. Indeed, he goes too far with the result that the sententious closing lines succeed only in recalling nineteenth-century verse at its most unattractive:

> Look on and jeer! Not Satan's thunder-quake
> Can cause the mighty walls of Heaven to shake
> As now they do, to hear a boy's heart break.

This cannot be meant seriously. To place such a ponderous weight of significance on such a trivial incident is plainly absurd, however characteristic of Victorian moralizing at its most grotesque. But, even if Betjeman's tongue was in his cheek as he wrote it, the poem can only be regarded as a successful parody of bad verse: in such a medium, failure is to be preferred to success.

Although both *Old Lights for New Chancels* and *New Bats in Old Belfries* appeared during the war, very few of the poems, directly or indirectly, reflect this fact. The war seemed to affect Betjeman as little as the political ferment of the thirties had done earlier. He was, of course, a non-combatant and was, for a couple of years, in neutral Dublin where the war must have seemed very far away. Of course, the Second World War did not produce much in the way of war poetry generally. There was no body of work, even from serving soldiers, to set beside that of Owen, Sorley, Graves, Sassoon and Rosenberg. There were several reasons for this: it was not felt this time that the conflict was senseless and futile, a chaotic muddle in which neither side could be said to be right and in which a callous older generation seemed intent on sacrificing its posterity on the altar of its own incompetence. It was rather felt that the war was

necessary and just and poems by soldiers on active service – Henry
Reed's 'Lessons of War', for instance – tended to reflect the comic
fatuities of military life rather than the physical horrors of battle.
There were far more opportunities to avoid actual fighting: the
question 'Where are the war poets?' could be answered with the neat
rejoinder, 'In the Ministry of Information.' But it was also a
civilians' war in another sense: the home front was often more
dangerous than the front line.

In so far as Betjeman had an attitude towards what was taking
place, it was one of regret for what was being destroyed as a direct
result of the war effort. He regretted the wanton destruction of
buildings and also, perhaps, the impending demise of a social system
which had started to totter in 1914 and had been delivered its death
blow in 1939. The elegiac note is detectable in 'Before Invasion,
1940' (originally called 'Anticipation in Spring'). It is a lament for
an England which had, in fact, vanished long before 1940.

> Still, fairly intact, and demolishing squads about,
> Bracketed station lamp with your oil-light taken away?
> Weep flowering currant, while your bitter cascades are out,
> Born in an age of railways, for flowering into to-day!

The aggressors here seem to be the men in the demolition squads
rather than the Luftwaffe. For Betjeman, the contemporary world
had always seemed irredeemable. The war was simply the ultimate
manifestation of twentieth-century barbarism. It had brought out
all the petty, organizing, bureaucratic busy-bodies, people whose
purpose in life was to instil uniformity and discipline, to stifle
individuality and creativity, and whose chief pleasure was the giving
of orders and the imposition of restrictions. He knew that such
people would delight in the destruction of the evidence of the past
symbolized by the old railway station which, humane and in-
efficient, could be shown to be irrelevant and dispensable in the
world of 'to-day!' (note the exclamation mark).

But Betjeman loved England passionately and, in 'Margate,
1940', he writes fondly of the cheap glitter of the seaside town and
simple fun of working-class holiday-makers temporarily cut short
by the war:

> Beside the Queen's Highcliffe now rank grows the vetch,
> Now dark is the terrace, a storm-battered stretch;

And I think, as the fairy-lit sights I recall,
It is those we are fighting for, foremost of all.

Although it is usual to accuse Betjeman of distaste for the lower
classes, he is certainly more sympathetic to the Margate trippers, a
cut-price crowd if ever there was one, than he is towards the middle-
class woman in 'In Westminster Abbey', whose hypocrisy and
snobbery are mercilessly exposed. She is not a nymph in whose
orisons anyone would wish to be remembered.

> Gracious Lord, oh bomb the Germans.
>   Spare their women for Thy Sake,
> And if that is not too easy
>   We will pardon Thy Mistake.
> But, gracious Lord, whate'er shall be,
> Don't let anyone bomb me.

The woman's prim litany of 'what our Nation stands for' –

> Books from Boots' and country lanes,
> Free speech, free passes, class distinction,
>   Democracy and proper drains

– may seem perilously close to Betjeman's own little Englandism
but there can be no doubt that he is aware of just how pathetic and
threadbare a catalogue it is. Whilst he has no great affection for this
poem himself, dismissing it as 'merely comic verse and competent
magazine writing', it gives the lie to critics who imagine that he is
soft on middle-class complacency. Furthermore, the sort of competence which it displays is not to be despised. It succeeds entirely
on its own terms, even if it seems slight when compared with his
very best poems.

A rather better piece of comedy from the same period and one
which is less narrowly topical, despite its solid foundation in the
circumstances of the war, is 'Invasion Exercise on the Poultry
Farm'. The setting is somewhat reminiscent of Lawrence's short
novel, *The Fox*; though Betjeman's treatment of the rural ménage
could not be more different. There is a strong narrative element in
the poem. It concludes with butch Marty Hayne, the lady poultry
farmer, taking cruel revenge on her friend Judy who has allowed
herself to be seduced al fresco by a deserting paratrooper. According
to the footnote, the poem was built round some unpromising lines

by a poet called Henry Oscar, one of those poets nobody but
Betjeman takes the trouble to read:

> Marty moves in dread towards the window – standing there
> Draws the curtain – sees the guilty movement of the pair.

To have invented a verse narrative, sharply characterized and
amusing, round two such banal lines is a triumph of ingenuity of
no small proportions, if a rather eccentric one.

The war did, of course, mean the loss of friends for Betjeman, as
for so many others. Friendship has always been particularly important to him with the result that he feels the death of loved ones with
acute sorrow and anguish. He wrote an elegy, 'In Memory of Basil,
Marquess of Dufferin and Ava' (his friend from Oxford, who was
killed on active service in Burma) which Lord Birkenhead considered to be 'of particular interest, for such was Betjeman's intense
grief at the loss of his friend, that for perhaps the first time in his
work he allows his own emotions to become evident in the poetry'.
Although the poem has also been admired by both Auden and
Donald Davie, it is by no means wholly satisfactory, despite – or,
perhaps, because of – the sonorous echoes of Arnold's marmoreal
elegies, such as 'In Rugby Chapel', and of Tennyson's *In Memoriam*.
In fact, there is a certain banality about the reiterated line – 'Friend
of my youth, you are dead!' – and the image of the Oxford pinnacles
standing motionless

> as though they too listened and waited
> Like me for your dear return

rather calls to mind those television commentators on royal occasions who like to endow the London statues with human emotions,
suggesting that they are somehow participating in the solemn
occasion. It is difficult today to write an elegy so mannered, so
formal, so dignified as this without seeming pompous and insincere.
Grief, when shrouded in eloquence, seems, however unjustly, to
call itself into question just as 'the articulate devotion', which Philip
Larkin once divined as the chief characteristic of the love poetry of
the past, seems to us faintly comic. It is a sign of how coarse our
sensibilities have become, perhaps.

> Stop, oh many bells, stop
> pouring on roses and creeper

Your unremembering peal
  this hollow, unhallowed V.E. Day, –
I am deaf to your notes and dead
  by a soldier's body in Burma.

While the harsh introduction of the corpse does something to lift
these lines above the level of plangent banality and while the
emotion behind them cannot be denied, there is something in the
manner (the histrionic summons to the bells, for instance) which
gives the poem a decidedly artificial and composed air from which
a modern sensibility recoils. Nor is the oppressively official manner
relieved by the personal references – 'sprawled on the southward
terrace', the 'Sports-Bugatti from Thame', 'Humorous, reckless,
loyal' – which conjure up a Dornford Yates hero rather than a real
man. Perhaps, the emotion was simply too raw to be transmuted
into art or Betjeman simply chose the wrong models, for elsewhere
he has written fine elegies which avoid the hackneyed, commem-
orative tone we encounter here.

    In addition to the poems already discussed, these two volumes
contain a few satirical poems. Unfortunately, they work no better
than the overtly satirical pieces in the two earlier collections. Betjeman
is effective and scores some palpable hits when he is gently unmasking
hypocrisy and snobbery, as he was in the lines on the middle-class
woman praying in Westminster Abbey or in 'Bristol and Clifton', an
equally devastating exposure of provincial pomposity and false piety.
He fails when his target is more generalized and nebulous – an idea,
for instance. In 'Group Life: Letchworth', where the target is social
progressiveness, he is to be seen at his worst:

> Barry's on the common far
>   Pedalling the Kiddie Kar.
> Ann has had a laxative
>   And Alured is dead.
> Sympathy is stencilling
>   Her decorative leatherwork,
> Wilfred's learned a folk-tune for
>   The Morris Dancers' band.

Betjeman's distaste for materialistic utopias is genuine enough,
though petulance rather than indignation seems to be the keynote
of this particular poem. The activities listed above seem innocuous,

if slightly silly. Even the crude interpolation, 'Alured is dead', fails
to suggest that there is a sinister side to this utopian simple-lifing,
though it is obviously intended to do so. The particular utopia
which Betjeman is describing is, furthermore, a thing of the past.
It is a William Morris-inspired earthly paradise with medieval
names, arts and crafts, 'Working each for weal of all'. Utopianism
had passed beyond this innocent stage at the time Betjeman wrote
the poem; people's justice was being dispensed in the Soviet Union,
a Welfare State was being fomented in liberal brains elsewhere. The
romantic fantasies of the Arts and Crafts movement had come to
seem ridiculous even to socialists. In *The Road to Wigan Pier* (1936)
Orwell issues a savage diatribe against precisely this kind of socialist
– the 'fruit juice drinker, nudist, sandal wearer, sex maniac, Quaker,
"Nature Cure" quack, pacifist and feminist' – which was, by an
interesting coincidence, occasioned by the sight of two grotesque
men in shorts getting on to a bus in Letchworth. But, by the
nineteen-forties, Orwell had come to see that the real enemy lay
elsewhere. Betjeman was, in fact, tilting at a target which had been
toppled long before and, what is more, by the other side. His thrusts
do not so much miss the target; it is simply that there is no target.

The same sort of confusion seems to be present in 'The Planster's
Vision' which takes as its subject those familiar Betjeman *bêtes noires*,
the planners, who wish to replace the unplanned untidiness, the
spirit of individualism which Betjeman upholds, with order and the
sense of community; to build a secure and soulless world planned
down to the last detail.

> I have a Vision of The Future, chum,
>   The workers' flats in fields of soya beans
>   Tower up like silver pencils, score on score:
> And Surging Millions hear the Challenge come
>   From microphones in communal canteens
>   'No Right! No Wrong! All's perfect, evermore.'

The vision of the past which Betjeman conjures up to set beside this
hideous future is a highly romantic one. He makes the planner cry,

> Remove those cottages, a huddled throng!
>   Too many babies have been born in there,
>   Too many coffins, bumping down the stair,
> Carried the old their garden paths along.

But, one asks, do planners really want to destroy old cottages? Don't they usually live in them? Aren't their activities usually confined to city centres and isn't Betjeman's real objection – and why not, of course – to the very idea of mass democracy: 'workers' flats', 'Surging Millions', 'communal canteens'? Hatred of mass democracy is nothing a poet need feel ashamed about; it is a legitimate poetic attitude and one shared by such gurus of the modern movement as Eliot, Yeats and Lawrence. But, to have force, it must be supported by something stronger than a liking for country cottages and 'moon-white church-towers' glimpsed through 'branches bare'. Betjeman's attack on the planners seems weak because it is founded only on misty-eyed nostalgia and sentiment; a picture postcard vision of what things seemed to look like once.

   Betjeman's concern for what we have learned to call the environment is, of course, deep and sincere; it is a subject he returns to in many poems. But he is more successful when he is expressing what he feels about places and their associations than when he is attacking those who would put our heritage in danger. In such poems he is guilty of perpetrating the kind of competent magazine writing of which he spoke in connection with 'In Westminster Abbey'. One such poem, though it is more accomplished and amusing than 'The Planster's Vision', is 'The Town Clerk's Views' which first appeared in *Selected Poems* (1948). The Town Clerk is one of Betjeman's ruthlessly efficient mandarins, puritanical and power-mad:

> He was, like all Town Clerks, from north of Trent;
> A man with bye-laws busy in his head
> Whose Mayor and Council followed where he led.
> His most capacious brain will make us cower,
> His only weakness is a lust for power –
> And that is not a weakness, people think,
> When unaccompanied by bribes or drink.

But it soon becomes clear that the Town Clerk is yet another Aunt Sally set up by Betjeman only in order to be knocked down. The description of a potentially dangerous official – a sort of municipal commissar or *gauleiter*, according to one's tastes – is effective and convincing. The litany of destruction which is buzzing in his brain is rather less so, however; if only because he is made to use the very same phrases to damn a place that Betjeman would use to praise it:

Those lumpy church towers, unadorned with spires,
And wavy roofs that burn like smouldering fires
In sharp spring sunlight over ashen flint
Are out of date as some old aquatint.
Then glance below the line of Sussex downs
To stucco terraces of seaside towns
Turn'd into flats and residential clubs
Above the wind-slashed Corporation shrubs.
Such Georgian relics should by now, I feel,
Be all rebuilt in glass and polished steel.

None knows better, or feels more strongly about it, than Betjeman how much municipal vandalism of this sort has gone on in our time. But one feels here that the Town Clerk is having words put in his mouth; the adjectives, the loving descriptions which preface the intention to destroy are Betjeman's and not his; with the result that, whilst we know what Betjeman means, we cannot believe that the Town Clerk is really such a monster if he has to be set up in this way. The cutting edge of the poem is blunted; the indignation, to an extent, neutralized; some sympathy has unwittingly been transferred to the intended victim of the satire.

Though Betjeman is not an accomplished satirist, he is a brilliant observer of the customs of the country. He has eyes and ears which pick up more than a whole team of social scientists. His poem 'Beside the Seaside' conjures up with a delicate mixture of irony and affection the whole atmosphere of an English seaside town at a particular point in history. It now seems rather dated, like a Donald McGill postcard, but the colours are still sharp and telling. It is a very long poem which comprehends a variety of moods: satirical observations; broad comedy; tragedy; lyrical description. As in Frith's painting of Ramsgate Sands, every square inch of surface is busy with detail; it is an achievement easier to describe than to analyse. In one of the best passages, Betjeman addresses himself in characteristic fashion to a very important subject:

Whether we like to sit with Penguin books
In sheltered alcoves farther up the cliff,
Or to eat winkles on the Esplanade,
Or to play golf along the crowded course,
Or on a twopenny borough council chair
To doze away the strains of *Humoresque*,

Adapted for the cornet and the drums
By the conductor of the Silver Band,
Whether we own a tandem or a Rolls,
Whether we Rudge it or we trudge it, still
A single topic occupies our minds.
'Tis hinted at or boldly blazoned in
Our accents, clothes and ways of eating fish,
And being introduced and taking leave,
'Farewell', 'So long', 'Bunghosky', 'Cheeribye' –
That topic all-absorbing, as it was,
Is now and ever shall be, to us – CLASS.

As should hardly need saying, Betjeman is not here being
snobbish or even mildly patronizing. He is simply reporting, with
unerring clarity, what he sees and hears. He is particularly sensitive
to the caste marks displayed by the English: a very tribal race, now
as then. There is the middle-class family whose daughter is
traumatized by Mr Pedder's neglect –

That life-long tragedy to Jennifer
Which ate into her soul and made her take
To secretarial work in later life
In a department of the Board of Trade

– with their Morris Eight, their suburban homestead, holidaying in
a hygienic, if rather restrictive, boarding-house. The stuffy Gros-
venor-Smiths, from a rather more prosperous section of the same
class, are no longer happy with the place they have been taking
childless holidays in for so many years:

'Not what it was, I'm very much afraid.
Look at that little mite with *Attaboy*
Printed across her paper sailor hat.
Disgusting, isn't it? Who *can* they be,
Her parents, to allow such forwardness?'

The working-class Browns, who are the offenders in this matter,
take a different view. Their holiday is the one high-point in lives of
unremitting, if well rewarded, toil and they enjoy themselves
uninhibitedly;

> But all the same they think the place 'Stuck up'
> And Blackpool, next year – if there *is* a next.

The whole poem adds up to a celebration of England or at least of one of her most characteristic features, the seaside town. It is a microcosm of English society and class – 'that topic all-absorbing' – is, for all its absurdity, the yeast which makes for richness and diversity. Against this miniature human community, full of petty shibboleths and taboos, unwritten codes of behaviour, the sea exists as it has always done, changeless and eternal, a symbol of permanence, 'consolingly disastrous', making the little vanities on display in the town seem trivial and silly indeed.

> And all the time the waves, the waves, the waves
> Chase, intersect and flatten on the sand
> As they have done for centuries, as they will
> For centuries to come, when not a soul
> Is left to picnic on the blazing rocks,
> When England is not England, when mankind
> Has blown himself to pieces. Still the sea,
> Consolingly disastrous, will return
> While the strange starfish, hugely magnified,
> Waits in the jewelled basin of a pool.

Despite the rather too lengthy digression about Mr Pedder and his antics early on in the poem, 'Beside the Seaside' is one of Betjeman's finest and most sustained achievements, with hardly a single false or jarring note. A whole chunk of English social history is mounted and preserved. Future generations wanting to know what England was like in the late nineteen-forties will ignore it at their peril.

Old Lights for New Chancels is subtitled 'Verses Topographical and Amatory'. The love poems, if such they can be called, have attracted much attention. In these amatory poems Betjeman nearly always adopts an oblique or sideways approach to the object of his devotion: he is the worshipper from afar, the supplicant who has to be humiliated or spurned by the Amazonian sports girl in whose arms he longs to be crushed. His fascination with large, muscular girls, though it is intended to amuse, must, equally obviously, answer some deep need in a nature in which a streak of masochism figures strongly. 'Pot Pourri from a Surrey Garden' (its title derived from Mrs C. W. Earle's almost forgotten handbook of household hints), outrageous and bizarrely rhymed as it is, illustrates this well. The voluptuous Amazon is pictured in her Surrey setting, a wild animal couched among the conifers. As her dubious charms are catalogued with perverse relish, we sense the dithyrambic throb of genuine passion:

> Pam, I adore you, Pam, you great big mountainous sports girl,
>   Whizzing them over the net, full of the strength of five:
> That old Malvernian brother, you zephyr and khaki shorts girl,
>   Although he's playing for Woking,
>   Can't stand up
> To your wonderful backhand drive.

Her physical attributes are likened to those of Hendren, the cricketer, rather than to those of a conventional female lovely and her attraction for the poet seems to lie partly in her pent-up ability to inflict pain so that he even envies the rhododendrons which she hacks at with her racket.

Miss Joan Hunter Dunn, the quintessential Betjeman woman, is rather less of a harridan than the formidable Pam. As in the earlier poem, despite the perversity and conscious farce, devotion is rewarded in the conventional way: marriage to Pam – 'Licensed now for embracement' – and engagement to Miss Hunter Dunn. Despite their undisciplined wildness, their thrilling physical presence, they are both – and this is certainly part of their attraction for Betjeman – nice, middle-class girls. Miss Hunter Dunn was, we are told, a real woman who worked as a canteen supervisor in the Ministry of Information and who was pointed out to Betjeman by Sir Kenneth Clark: an introduction which Clark considers to be his 'most lasting achievement' as Director of the Films Division. While Miss Hunter Dunn is a pretty, outdoor girl rather than an intimidating virago, Betjeman once again assumes the role of an inferior: weak, supplicatory, perhaps rather despised:

> Miss Joan Hunter Dunn, Miss Joan Hunter Dunn,
> How mad I am, sad I am, glad that you won.
> The warm-handled racket is back in its press,
> But my shock-headed victor, she loves me no less.

Although it describes a real girl, Betjeman feels that he must play a part in order to express his admiration and pleasure. It is the subaltern and not Betjeman who gets the girl. The poet woos his beloved, as it were, by proxy. Her attraction is not only physical: she is a sort of idealized denizen of the lush Surrey landscape, with its tennis courts and pine plantations and comfortable suburban houses, 'Furnish'd and burnish'd by Aldershot sun'. In fact, her rich suburban habitat is reminiscent of 'Love in a Valley' and the poem may almost be read as a sequel to that earlier work, the 'Portable Lieutenant' returned, at last, to claim his prize. The entrancing metre, the sly humour, the charming descriptive touches are all satisfying. The irony, however, which offsets the real passion on which the poem is founded is, in the end, rather troubling. As this was a real girl in a real place, Betjeman's wilful transformation of her into an object of fantasy, who may only be approached by means of an elaborate disguise, seems irritatingly adolescent and uncalled for.

This emotional infantilism, if such it may be called, can be rather embarrassing, as in the two poems about 'Myfanwy'. But it ensures that his poems about pre-pubertal love – 'Indoor Games near Newbury', for instance – have a truthfulness and intensity, an absence of whimsical affectation, which is unique. The sort of childish passions –

> Love so pure it *had* to end,
> Love so strong that I was frighten'd
> When you gripped my fingers tight and
> Hugging, whispered 'I'm your friend.'

– described there are still real to him so that he can write about them without seeming arch. In 'North Coast Recollections' he writes about calf love with an adult awareness of the transitoriness of such emotions which yet makes no attempt to belittle their once overwhelming seriousness:

> First love so deep, John Lambourn cannot speak,
> So deep, he feels a tightening in his throat,
> So tender, he could brush away the sand
> Dried up in patches on her freckled legs,
> Could hold her gently till the stars went down,
> And if she cut herself would staunch the wound,
> Yes, even with this First Eleven scarf,
> And hold it there for hours.

Lines such as these (though the dull-minded might object that John

Lambourn is merely a projection of the clean-limbed public school heroes who figured in the pages of *Gem* and *Magnet*) honestly express real adolescent longing as it was once experienced.

As well as the famous poems such as 'Pot Pourri from a Surrey Garden', and 'A Subaltern's Love-song', which has attained a sort of minor classic status, leading Betjeman to describe it as his 'signature tune', Betjeman has produced other love poems which are equally satisfying in their own strange way. 'An Archaeological Picnic' justly found its way into the anthology of *English Love Poems* which Betjeman co-edited with Geoffrey Taylor. It is eccentric but also deeply personal in a way which the other and better-known poems, where Betjeman is playfully indulging a conscious poetic attitude, are not.

> In this high pasturage, this Blunden time,
>   With Lady's Finger, Smokewort, Lovers' Loss,
> And lin-lan-lone a Tennysonian chime
>   Stirring the sorrel and the gold-starred moss,
>   Cool is the chancel, bright the altar cross.
>
> Drink, Mary, drink your fizzy lemonade
>   And leave the king-cups; take your grey felt hat;
> Here, where the low-side window lends a shade,
>   There, where the key lies underneath the mat,
>   The rude forefathers of the hamlet sat.

The poem succeeds without recourse to any of the faintly disturbing nursery *kitsch* which characterizes the two poems about Myfanwy. It remains, however, obstinately unusual: a love poem in which the architecture of a church is more sharply realized than the girl. One is reminded of the extraordinary letter which Pugin sent to a friend announcing his second marriage and explaining that he had 'got a first rate Gothic woman at last, who perfectly delights in spires, chancels, screens, stained windows, brasses, vestments, etc.' Betjeman would have sympathized with the Victorian architect's undisguised pleasure at such a find; poor Mary seems to have preferred her fizzy lemonade.

In that strange, compelling poem, 'The Irish Unionist's Farewell to Greta Hellstrom in 1922', Betjeman, almost for the first time, seems to be speaking the language of adult passion:

> Golden haired and golden hearted
>   I would ever have you be,
> As you were when last we parted
>   Smiling slow and sad at me.
> Oh! the fighting down of passion!
>   Oh! the century-seeming pain –
> Parting in this off-hand fashion
>   In Dungarvan in the rain.

Although the title remains baffling, there is a virile energy about these lines which makes them very different from anything of this sort which Betjeman had previously attempted.

One of his most pleasing poems, 'Youth and Age on Beaulieu River, Hants', is both topographical and amatory; the beauty of the landscape and of the girl, as she rows her craft on the river, blend; the girl becoming a sort of wraith-like emanation of the natural beauty which surrounds her. The poem has an exquisite lyricism and delicacy which makes it as satisfying as anything which Betjeman has written.

> Tulip figure, so appealing,
>   Oval face, so serious-eyed,
> Tree-roots pass'd and muddy beaches.
> On to huge and lake-like reaches,
>   Soft and sun-warm, see her glide –
> Slacks the slim young limbs revealing,
> Sun-brown arm the tiller feeling –
>   With the wind and with the tide.

Though the poem celebrates the combination of youth and beauty, bodied forth in the exquisite girl as in the fresh, clean summer landscape, it is also aware of the lurking shadow: the light of evening waiting to close over the landscape; loneliness and old age, which has already claimed the sad Mrs Fairclough who sighs at the sight of so much confidence and beauty, waiting for the girl:

> Evening light will bring the water,
>   Day-long sun will burst the bud,
> Clemency, the General's daughter,
>   Will return upon the flood.
> But the older woman only

Knows the ebb-tide leaves her lonely
  With the shining fields of mud.

In 'Senex', Betjeman subjects his interest in pretty girls to ironic
scrutiny. He pictures himself as a voyeuristic cruiser ('At sundown
on my tricycle /I tour the Borough's edge'), assailed by temptation
on every side, like a latterday St Antony, though his tormentors
assume a more attractive form:

Get down from me! I thunder there,
  You spaniels! Shut your jaws!
Your teeth are stuffed with underwear
Suspenders torn asunder there
  And buttocks in your paws!

Significantly enough the dogs are not ferocious hounds but rather
spaniels, dogs noted for their docility and playfulness. The
humour rests in the reader's awareness that, whilst the poet cries
out to be rid of his lust ('Oh whip the dogs away my Lord'), his
interest in girls is as harmless and playful as the spaniels themselves.
There is also the inevitable disparity between intention and achievement for, as he prays for release from sin, the objects of his desire
('bare knees', 'sulky lips') continue to assert themselves despite his
furious disavowals:

Oh whip the dogs away my Lord,
  They make me ill with lust.
Bend bare knees down to pray, my Lord,
Teach sulky lips to say, my Lord,
  That flaxen hair is dust.

Betjeman's pleas for deliverance from the sins of the flesh and the
'merry misery' to which they reduce him is not to be taken too
seriously. His terror of death, however, is. This darker side of
Betjeman's nature is revealed, for the first time, in two powerful and
moving poems in which he expresses direct emotion without resort
to evasive irony or elaborately constructed personae. 'On a Portrait
of a Deaf Man' is about the poet's father and, unlike the elegy for his
friend Lord Dufferin, deep feeling and grief are sufficiently distanced
to make possible a completely satisfying and profound work of art.
Memories of the dead man are punctuated by – or, rather, detonate

– grim reflections on the corpse's physical decay as it lies in the
ground. Remembering the 'loosely fitting shooting clothes' which
his father affected in life brings to mind the 'closely fitting shroud'
in which he was buried. Memories of the country walks they went
on when he was a boy prompt the reflection,

> And when he could not hear me speak
>   He smiled and looked so wise
> That now I do not like to think
>   Of maggots in his eyes.

The gloom of this poem and the morbid dwelling on the physical
accidents of death are reminiscent of Betjeman's beloved Hardy, and
John Wain has plausibly remarked that the poem 'would probably
not have come out quite as it did if Hardy had never existed'. It
certainly represents a more sombre Betjeman than we have seen
hitherto and introduces what were later to become almost stock
properties – the tombs of Highgate Cemetery, its 'soaked Carrara-
covered earth /For Londoners to fill' – and the question of religious
doubt – 'You ask me to believe You and /I only see decay' – which
is more powerfully treated in the second of these poems.

'Before the Anaesthetic' deals memorably with Betjeman's own
fear of death and physical pain. As he lies in his hospital bed, St
Giles's bells are ringing out for him but seem to contain no promise
of peace or comforting hope of salvation:

> Intolerably sad and true,
> Victorian red and jewel blue,
> The mellow bells are ringing round
> And charge the evening light with sound . . .

However, even when he is at his most serious, he is unable to resist
a self-conscious (and self-defeating) joke as when he points out that
'jewel blue' is taken from Rumer Godden. It is as if, wary of too
much solemnity, he wishes to signal to the reader: 'Don't take all
this agonizing too seriously. I am still up to my old tricks.'
Fortunately, the crassly intrusive footnote, which many editors have
chosen to omit, does not seriously damage the poem, which builds
up to a pitch of emotional intensity never attempted previously.
The authentic cry of anguish, denuded of any extraneous self-
mockery, is heard with a sense of shock, as if one were hearing a
dumb child speak for the first time.

> Is it extinction when I die?
> I move my limbs and use my sight;
> Not yet, thank God, not yet the Night.

Betjeman's fear of death, the strongest emotion in his entire being, springs from the shakiness of his religious belief, the failure of his wish to believe to be reinforced by faith, and his sense of personal unworthiness. He is terrified 'that this "I" should cease to be' because he feels, at this critical moment, '*I never knew the Lord at all*'.

> Illuminated missals – spires –
> Wide screens and decorated quires –
> All these I loved, and on my knees
> I thanked myself for knowing these . . .

His aesthetic pleasure in church architecture and ecclesiastical ritual, his self-congratulatory delight in the minuteness of his knowledge of these things seems now vain and even sinful, as he contemplates death at close quarters. As he lies on the bed, he realizes,

> Almighty Saviour, had I Faith,
> There'd be no fight with kindly Death.

Would that he could share Donne's certainty: 'Death be not proud . . . one short sleep past, we wake eternally.' That he cannot is a personal tragedy for Betjeman; though it has produced a poem which ranks among the finest he has written.

In 'Before the Anaesthetic', Betjeman's doubt and fear supply a dramatic tension which animates the whole poem. This dramatic tension between the poet's chaotic fears and the impulse to order and arrange which is central to making a work of art is absent from those poems in which he celebrates and affirms his love for the Church of England. These do not always avoid a tone of bland moral smugness. The expression of certainty is less convincing in a modern poet than it is in a seventeenth-century divine, well acquainted with the darker side of life. However, in 'A Lincolnshire Church' in which Betjeman enters a church in the spirit of an Anglican communicant and expert on church architecture, one who definitely knows whether the roof has been cleaned or restored, unlike Philip Larkin's puzzled agnostic in 'Church Going', he achieves a poem of this sort which manages not to be dull; perhaps because of the unexpected appearance of the Indian Christian priest

right at the end of the poem. It is not, however, the liturgical
eloquence –

> There where the white light flickers
> By the white and silver veil,
> A wafer dipped in a wine-drop
> Is the Presence the angels hail

– which stays in the mind so much as the picture of grey, post-war England, in which austerity and hopelessness are the order of the day and
whose drab evidences wash against the stranded church like flotsam:

> And around it, turning their backs,
> The usual sprinkle of villas;
> The usual woman in slacks,
> Cigarette in her mouth,
> Regretting Americans, stands
> As a wireless croons in the kitchen,
> Manicuring her hands.
> Dear old, bloody old England
> Of telegraph poles and tin,
> Seemingly so indifferent
> And with so little soul to win.

Another and more impressive poem of religious affirmation,
tinged with melancholy and regret for what the present has done to
England, is about a church which has personal associations for
Betjeman, 'St Saviour's, Aberdeen Park, Highbury, London, N.'.
It has claims to be regarded as one of his best poems, technically
confident and impressively serious. Poems such as this and 'Before
the Anaesthetic' point the direction in which Betjeman's verse was
to go. The 'great Victorian church, tall, unbroken and bright', now
stands in the wasteland of post-war north London: an area scarred
by derelict plots of land, threaded by trolley-buses, its houses
dilapidated and turned over to flats. Though the place is much
changed, Betjeman still feels a sense of belonging, for this is the
part of London where he has his roots:

> These were the streets my parents knew when they loved and
> won –
> The brougham that crunched the gravel, the laurel-girt paths
> that wind,

Geranium-beds for the lawn, Venetian blinds for the sun,
  A separate tradesman's entrance, straw in the mews behind,
Just in the four-mile radius where hackney carriages run,
  Solid Italianate houses for the solid commercial mind.

In the safe Victorian world, so precisely and appreciatively realized, the church was solidly grounded in traditional beliefs and honest values. It is a world to which Betjeman still feels a deep loyalty. As he kneels in 'the stencilled chancel', characteristically aware of his architectural as well as his spiritual location, he feels God's presence in the very place his parents once worshipped; he is moved by this continuity and expresses it in a magnificent peroration:

Wonder beyond Time's wonders, that Bread so white and small
  Veiled in golden curtains, too mighty for men to see,
Is the Power which sends the shadows up this polychrome wall,
  Is God who created the present, the chain-smoking
                                   millions and me;
Beyond the throb of the engines is the throbbing heart of all –
Christ, at this Highbury altar, I offer myself To Thee.

Bernard Bergonzi considers that the reference to 'the chain-smoking millions and me' suggests that 'even in the presence of God [Betjeman] is unable to feel secure without consciously assuring himself of his separation from the masses outside'. But Betjeman is aware that he, as much as the chain-smoking millions, is lost in the wasteland of the present. He believes that the fact of Christ's resurrection alone offers the hope of dignity and meaning in this life; the promise of eternal salvation in the next. It is in a spirit of unity and not of division that he offers himself as he kneels before the altar. He cannot be anything other than alone when he is communicating directly with God and it is this inevitable and essential loneliness before his creator which, *pace* Professor Bergonzi, accounts for his separation of himself from the millions outside rather than simple snobbery. As the poem clearly states, God created the poet *and* the chain-smoking millions as well as the beastly present in which both are condemned to live: they are brothers under the skin. It is an impressive poem which, when compared with 'Hymn' from *Mount Zion*, shows how far Betjeman had come within the space of little more than a decade.

CHAPTER FOUR

CLAY AND SPIRIT

A Few Late Chrysanthemums (1954), together with some of the additional poems included in the 1958 edition of *Collected Poems*, represents the summit of Betjeman's poetic achievement. Even the best poems in the two war-time collections had not prepared readers for the sustained excellence of the poems in this slim volume; particularly for those in the section called 'Gloom' which express, honestly and directly, emotions only glimpsed through a veil of evasive irony in the earlier poems. The authentically personal note present in only a few of those poems – 'On a Portrait of a Deaf Man' or 'Before the Anaesthetic' – is fully audible here. The depth of feeling, the compassion, the sensitivity to the pathos of submerged lives which was merely a lurking presence in a poem such as, say, 'Death in Leamington', whose gaily ironic surface camouflaged the genuine emotional core of the poem, emerge into full daylight. Poem after poem deals with the major themes: love and the loss of love, death, guilt and religious doubt. What had previously been obscured by mannerisms, by eccentricities of metre, by perversities of taste and feeling, by the apparent whimsicality of private interests is now clearly and movingly articulated. As John Press observed, such a performance should have 'dispelled any lingering doubt that Betjeman was not a serious artist'. Certainly, it should no longer have been contestable that he was merely an entertaining light versifier. It was, as Geoffrey Taylor remarked in *Time and Tide*, 'rather as though something friendly, familiar and furry and easily frightened had turned at bay and bitten one in the bathroom'.

In an article in the *Spectator* (8 October 1954), Betjeman reviewed his reviewers. He threw much incidental light on his method of writing and on the mood which had produced these fine mature poems: 'When most of the poems in my latest collection were written, I was the self-pitying victim of remorse, guilt and terror of death.' Certainly these dark emotions – though not always accompanied by self-pity – are present in the best of these poems. Their source seems to be Betjeman's troubled Christian conscience, wanting to believe yet constantly afflicted by doubt and the promptings of the flesh. His agonized awareness of the impossibly high standard set by Jesus Christ makes him intolerably aware of his own shortcomings. A burden of guilt, already heavy, is made heavier during these years by memories of his lack of duty towards his parents and by present awareness of the lack of consideration which he has shown for his wife. He is haunted by the transitoriness of earthly existence and terrified by the prospect of extinction, his own and that of his friends. It was at this time that he told Kenneth Allsop that he thought about death every day. His fear of death, like his sense of guilt, can be attributed to the uncertainty of his faith: a telling illustration of the sad truth that religious beliefs, to all save the most complacent souls, are more often the cause of acute suffering than it is of cosy well-being.

In general, these mature poems are more directly about people and less about places; though a place is often still the point of departure for a particular poem. While in 'Love in a Valley', the poet's attention is caught by the pines and rhododendrons of suburban Surrey, the girl in effect becoming just another natural feature of the landscape, in a later poem, 'Felixstowe', although characterized by similarly precise observation, the figure in the foreground, in this case an old nun, is neither subordinate to her setting nor merely expressive of it. There is no archness in Betjeman's presentation of her tragedy. We no longer need to wonder whether we should laugh or cry because Betjeman feels no need to conceal his own heartfelt response by the application of surface whimsicality.

These mature poems show that John Sparrow's view of Betjeman as 'a landscape poet' was only an interim judgement. 'Greenaway' is about the poet's own inner torments rather than about Cornwall; just as 'Norfolk' and 'Hertfordshire' are about adult feelings of guilt and nostalgia for lost innocence rather than about the places from which their titles derive. If one compares either of these poems with, say, 'Parliament Hill Fields', one notes that in the earlier poem Betjeman is simply recording a memory, stating how it was for one of his age and class at that particular moment. In the later poem, he is surveying childhood from the standpoint of troubled middle age, not liking what he sees, regretting the past and posing difficult questions: 'How did the Devil come? When first attack?' Such direct questions were, in a sense, the unspoken subtext to such nostalgic reveries as 'Parliament Hill Fields'. One senses the real pain behind the rapt contemplation of the scenes of childhood, but only in these later poems does Betjeman feel able to put such questions openly and clearly.

The increased seriousness means that the poems are, for the most part, profoundly sad. The recurrent themes are fear of death and dying, nostalgia for a vanished past, loneliness, his own and that of others, loss, failure and remorse. Life's sadness rather than its joys – of which Betjeman showed himself, however, to be still appreciative in a few poems – is certainly the theme of what are perhaps the three best poems in *A Few Late Chrysanthemums*: 'Middlesex', 'The Metropolitan Railway' and 'The Old Liberals'.

The first of these is a very familiar piece, being one of Betjeman's most anthologized poems. It is a lament for the departed rural world now engulfed by London's spreading suburbs as well as a condemnation of the vapid consumerism of the present, which is compared with the simple certainties of the past. The first two stanzas are mildly satirical about 'Fair Elaine the bobby-soxer', a typical modern girl coming home to Ruislip Gardens station after a day at the office, intent only on sandwich supper and the television screen. She is presented in terms of the branded products which she uses – Windsmoor overcoat, Jacqmar scarf, Drene and Innoxa cosmetics – all of which serve to place her socially as well as to denote her spiritual vacancy. In the third stanza, this *vers de société* mood changes and the poet recalls Middlesex as it once was. This transition has been considered abrupt and disconcerting though it is, in fact, sign-posted in the earlier reference to the 'few surviving hedges' which, amid the concrete and the other tawdry signs of progress, 'keep alive our lost Elysium – rural Middlesex again'. Betjeman's evocation of this vanished rural paradise is elegiac in tone; though the references to particular places, the characteristic precision of observation – trees are not just trees but elms or laburnums – assure us that it is not an idealized vision of the past which is being conjured up but a once real place. This Middlesex is remembered

with sharp pictorial clarity as well as deep love; we sense a feeling
of deep personal loss.

> Gentle Brent, I used to know you
> Wandering Wembley-wards at will,
> Now what change your waters show you
> In the meadowlands you fill!
> Recollect the elm-trees misty
> And the footpaths climbing twisty
> Under cedar-shaded palings,
> Low laburnum-leaned-on railings,
> Out of Northolt on and upward to the heights
> of Harrow hill.

In the final stanza we are poignantly reminded that this once
beautiful landscape has vanished as completely as its former inhabitants whose innocence and simplicity contrasts with 'Fair Elaine's'
shallowness and pseudo-sophistication:

> Cockney anglers, cockney shooters,
> Murray Poshes, Lupin Pooters,
> Long in Kensal Green and Highgate silent under
> soot and stone.

The significance of this final reference to characters from the
Grossmiths' *The Diary of a Nobody*, one of Betjeman's favourite
books, is made clearer in another poem, 'Thoughts on *The Diary of
a Nobody*', in which, thinking of their unfortunate trip to Watney
Lodge, he addresses the Pooters directly:

> Dear Charles and Carrie, I am sure,
> Despite that awkward Sunday dinner,
> Your lives were good and more secure
> Than ours at cocktail time in Pinner.

'The Metropolitan Railway' is unmarked by the social snobbery,
the hint of condescension which could be objected to in 'Middlesex'.
An unsympathetic critic might dismiss that poem as the work of a
rich Edwardian regretting the elevation of the masses and miss the
plangent registering of a loss which is everyone's, Elaine's as much
as the poet's. 'The Metropolitan Railway' is not nostalgic in the
same way, though it recalls the past with a similar feeling of regret.
Its focus is more precise; it records the particular sadness of

individual lives rather than a generalized sense of loss. It is about shattered illusions, the false scent of hope which animates unimportant lives before they are finally extinguished. The station buffet at Baker Street with its rich Victorian furnishings was built with the same 'radiant hope' that a young Edwardian couple invested in building their life together. The station was their meeting-place after days of work in the City or days of shopping in Oxford Street. They were young; their world seemed safe and secure as well as fresh and new, radiant with hope and full of promise. They were sanguine, at home in the optimistic age in which they lived, an age in which everything seemed settled and yet in which everything seemed possible:

> They felt so sure on their electric trip
> That Youth and Progress were in partnership.

But such unthinking happiness could not last; their sort of progress was succeeded by another sort which held no place for them: hope died before they did:

> Cancer has killed him. Heart is killing her.
>   The trees are down. An Odeon flashes fire
> Where stood their villa by the murmuring fir
>   When 'they would for their children's good conspire.'
> Of all their loves and hopes on hurrying feet
> Thou art the worn memorial, Baker Street.

Betjeman is here saying something more than that things and places outlast us: he is saying that they are witnesses of the lives which are lived within them. It is this sense of places being a part of the texture of our lives which underlies Betjeman's interest in architecture. Kingsley Amis expressed something of the same sort when he wrote apropos of 'Aberdarcy: the Main Square':

> All love demands a witness: something 'there'
> Which it yet makes part of itself.

The objects in the station buffet which Betjeman describes so knowledgeably and lovingly in the first stanza are not there merely as local colour or period detail but rather because for Betjeman, as for the couple whose tragedy is the subject of the poem, they are charged with a deep emotional significance. In 'Monody on the Death of Aldersgate Street Station', the same feeling is present with the result that the imminent destruction of the building is registered with the same sense of personal loss that is communicated in Betjeman's elegies for dead friends. Buildings are more than heaps of brick and stone and their loss is irreparable and heartrending. This feeling that our surroundings contain us, are visible symbols of our pathetic hopes and aspirations, is a feature of his prose writing about architecture as much as it is of his poems.

'The Old Liberals', like 'The Metropolitan Railway', is about people whose lives have been built on illusion; as, to an extent, all lives are. However, their regret is not just for a world which is past but rather for one which never really was. A father and daughter, relics of the age of William Morris and the reforming spirit which flowed through the Church of England at the beginning of the century, play one of the Yattendon hymns on *hautbois* and recorder in their Boar's Hill retreat. Their music-making strikes Betjeman as hopelessly sad, a poignant reminder of the transcience of hope:

> I think such a running together of woodwind sound,
> Such painstaking piping high on a Berkshire hill,
> Is sad as an English autumn heavy and still,
> Sad as a country silence, tractor-drowned;
> For deep in the hearts of the man and the woman playing
> The rose of a world that was not has withered away.

Their belief in a world of happy rural content supported by honest faith has proved illusory, leaving them lost and bewildered in the trough of an unsympathetic age:

> Where are the free folk of England? Where are they?

The world which never was, conjured up in the romantic-archaic words ('the wains with garlanded swathes a-swaying', 'the blithe and jocund to ted the hay') has been succeeded by the all-too-real trash of today. The 'free folk of England' have dispersed into suburbs served by cinemas and fish and chip shops. The music piping on the hill is a sort of requiem for a world which was never more than a pious dream, an affecting reminder of what might have been; its beauty and haunting sadness contrasting with a brash materialist present which cannot even understand the completeness of its loss:

> Here amid firs and a final sunset flare
> Recorder and *hautbois* only moan at a mouldering sky.

In other poems in this collection, Betjeman writes about the
personal tragedy of the lonely, the neglected, the uncompanioned.
'Business Girls' manages to be both funny and sad without appearing
to belittle the pathetic human flotsam which it describes. It is
expressive of his sensitivity to place – in this case Camden Town
with its large Victorian houses divided into bedsitters – as well as
his sympathy for human outcasts.

> From the geyser ventilators
>   Autumn winds are blowing down
> On a thousand business women
>   Having baths in Camden Town.

Betjeman is aware that these dull, unfulfilled spinsters are comic but
he senses the sadness at the centre of their empty lives: no husband
or children to care; no proper home to come back to; only a ticket-
of-leave existence and the dull round of a monotonous job; a life as
devoid of comfort as it is of love.

> Rest you there, poor unbelov'd ones,
>   Lap your loneliness in heat.
> All too soon the tiny breakfast,
>   Trolley-bus and windy street!

In 'Eunice' he gives a close-up, as it were, of one of these women.
He has said that he wrote this poem after seeing a woman waiting
on the platform of Tunbridge Wells Central with flowers in her
hand and trying to imagine what might have brought her there. It
is a method of approach more typical of the novelist than the poet.
Nevertheless the poem succeeds entirely as a portrait of a particular
person, with each detail – the 'cream and green and cosy' flat high
in Onslow Gardens, the little hutment in Kent, the typing job in
London (though one wonders if she would not have been more
likely to be a middle-grade civil servant than a typist) –
chosen with a connoisseur's eye for the minutiae of ordinary lives.
It is also a study of loneliness and the loss of love, for Betjeman
attributes Eunice's air of abandoned sadness to the effects of an
unhappy love affair.

In 'House of Rest', he writes about a vicar's widow, surrounded
by the little relics of her unimportant life. He appreciates them with
the eye of a practised ecclesiastical observer – he knows, for instance,
that the photograph of Lincoln Cathedral is by Valentine and Co.

– as well as a sympathetic understanding of the poignancy of their associations for their owner. He does not appear as an ecclesiastical voyeur, as he might have done in an earlier poem. In fact, he consciously checks his church-bibber's curiosity:

> I do not like to ask if he
>   Was 'High' or 'Low' or 'Broad'
> Lest such a question seem to be
>   A mockery of Our Lord.

Such 'mockery' was never far from the surface in the early poems and 'House of Rest', though not one of his best poems, shows how far he had come. It is all too easy to imagine how the younger Betjeman would have lingered over the surface detail, relishing its quaintness, poking gentle fun at the husband's theological 'position' and, in the process, hiding his own true feelings.

In 'Felixstowe, *or* The Last of Her Order', one of the several poems which first appeared in book form in *Collected Poems*, he achieves a poem of great poignancy and delicacy which ranks among his very best. The loneliness of the old nun, the last of the Little Sisters of the Hanging Pyx, is of a different sort from that of the business girls in Camden Town because it is warmed by the certainty of faith. Her remote setting, the dim seaside town on the east coast, is beautifully evoked in the first stanza:

> With one consuming roar along the shingle
>   The long wave claws and rakes the pebbles down
> To where its backwash and the next wave mingle,
>   A mounting arch of water weedy-brown
> Against the tide the off-shore breezes blow.
>   Oh wind and water, this is Felixstowe.

The isolated little town, buffeted by sea and wind, images the endurance of the faithful nun who accepts her own isolation with an almost humorous resignation:

> I put my final shilling in the meter
> And only make my loneliness completer.

She does not repine that now only she is 'left to keep the rule'. She feels 'Safe with the Love that I was born to know': happy, secure and content. Her life is full in a way which Eunice's and the business girls' are not. She does not need, and so is able to dismiss, 'the vain

world's silly sympathizing' because she is secure in the knowledge
of God's love. But her sense of well-being is neither smug nor
complacent. Her exile is voluntary and her life has purpose. Such
solitude is by no means the same as loneliness. Indeed, in her patient
perseverance in a rule which means nothing to the age into which
she has survived, there is a sort of heroism.

Betjeman himself, of course, knows no such certainty and there
are several poems which deal memorably with his fear of death.
One of the best of these is 'Devonshire Street W.1' which, because
it is not about his own death, avoids the self-pity which spoils some
of the other poems. It captures, with painful clarity, the moment
when the imminence of death is first apprehended. The handsome
eighteenth-century houses in this doctors' quarter of London stand,
'lofty and calm', neutral bystanders, indifferent and bland before
the fact of death, their dignified self-possession deepening the dying
man's sense of isolation as he emerges with the fatal X-rays under
his arm.

> No hope. And the iron knob of this palisade
>   So cold to the touch, is luckier now than he
> 'Oh merciless, hurrying Londoners! Why was I made
>   For the long and the painful deathbed coming to me?'

It is, however, the wife's timid gesture of sympathy which moves
us more than the husband's anguished cry; proving, as Philip Larkin
puts it: 'Our almost-instinct almost true: /What will survive of us is
love'.

> She puts her fingers in his as, loving and silly,
>   At long-past Kensington dances she used to do
> 'It's cheaper to take the tube to Piccadilly
>   And then we can catch a nineteen or a twenty-two.'

Betjeman is not saying anything so trite as, 'But life goes on'; he is
affirming his faith in the strength of human love which reveals itself
in the simple rather than the grand gesture and recognizing, once
again, that there is a heroism in quite ordinary lives.

The couple in 'Devonshire Street W.1' could be the couple in
'The Metropolitan Railway'. In fact, this dovetailing of one poem
into another is very characteristic: 'Eunice' and 'Business Girls';
'Middlesex' and 'Thoughts on *The Diary of a Nobody*'; 'Love in a
Valley' and 'A Subaltern's Love-song'. Betjeman has created a

genuine country of the mind which is, as Lord David Cecil said, as recognizable, as emotionally charged and as self-contained as Hardy's Wessex. It is a sad world in which the apparently insignificant assumes significance, in which lives are defined by unimportant things such as the shops in a typical high street. In 'Variation on a Theme by T. W. Rolleston' the tragedy of a woman's death is perceived through such 'unimportant' things. The poem is, incidentally, a parody of a poem by Rolleston, a minor Irish poet, called 'The Dead at Clonmacnois' which evokes, in fine Celtic fashion, the roll-call of the honoured dead – the warriors of Erin and the kings of Tara – an ironic contrast with the more humble roll-call sounded here:

> But her place is empty in the queue at the International,
>   The greengrocer's queue lacks one,
> So does the crowd at MacFisheries. There's no one to go to
>   Freeman's
>   To ask if the shoes are done.

Though this is certainly not one of Betjeman's best poems, it is important to understand that he is being neither snobbish nor patronizing in rehearsing this pathetic litany. He recognizes that the shop names are landmarks in the landscape of a particular existence, defining fragments of a life like the Nineteen and the Twenty-Two. Such things, dull and trivial in themselves, are significant in the context of an individual life. Though, elsewhere, Betjeman might regret their brash intrusiveness in a village street, he here acknowledges their place in a simple life which takes much of its meaning from such things.

In 'I. M. Walter Ramsden', Betjeman's most moving elegy, on the death of an old science don at Pembroke, Oxford, that obscure little college of which Betjeman is so fond, he produces a poem of great technical originality; a noteworthy achievement from a writer who generally prefers to take the metrical framework of a poem, as it were, from stock. The tone is measured and calm, as befits an elegy: long rhyming lines alternate with disyllabic ones which have the effect almost of pauses in a slow march:

> Dr Ramsden cannot read *The Times* obituary to-day
> He's dead.

Let monographs on silk worms by other people be
     Thrown away
     Unread
For he who best could understand and criticize them, he
     Lies clay
     In bed.

The very plainness of this is affecting in a way that the more high-flown manner of the lines about Lord Dufferin is not. It is not only an obscure individual who is being mourned but a past age, as in the poem about George V. Dr Ramsden leaves behind not just his silkworms but memories which now only a handful of old friends share as they recall long Edwardian afternoons. This simpler world, with which Dr Ramsden formed a link, is more completely lost with his death. His friends feel closer to death themselves now that he has left them; haunted by memories of 'the long-dead generations' who preceded him on the long journey.

Betjeman is painfully aware that the skull is for ever grinning behind the apparently healthy flesh, a constant *memento mori*. In the elegy for Dr Ramsden he pictures the pink cheeks 'drain'd white' in death, while in the earlier 'On a Portrait of a Deaf Man' the imagery of death – maggots in the eyes, finger-bones sticking through finger-ends – assumes a positively Beddoes-like horridness. In 'St Cadoc', which dates from the same period, Betjeman had meditated gloomily, not to say morbidly, on his own death, imagining the tree growing somewhere from which his coffin would be cut and thinking of the worms which would consume his body once it was interred.

'Before the Anaesthetic' had dealt with Betjeman's immediate fear of death without recourse to these Grand Guignol effects. In 'The Cottage Hospital', from *A Few Late Chrysanthemums*, he appears almost to be rewriting that poem. He contemplates his own inevitable end with the same self-tormenting horror and undisguised dread though, on this occasion, he seems less plagued by religious guilt than by fear of actual physical pain. In fact, Betjeman seems helpless to protect himself from these compulsive images of death. Although this poem is often regarded as one of his best, its lack of restraint seems almost a flaw; especially when compared with Philip Larkin's 'The Building', also about a hospital. In Larkin's magnificent poem, the building is surveyed dispassionately, its terrible purpose emerging slowly but inevitably. Larkin is the observer, watching 'Humans caught on ground curiously neutral'; implicated in their fate but also detached. Like the people in the hospital, he knows he is going to die but he is stoical and resigned, unlike Betjeman, who says outright what Larkin's frightened and trapped humans are thinking, or perhaps trying not to think:

> Say in what Cottage Hospital
>   whose pale green walls resound
> With the tap upon polished parquet
>   of inflexible nurses' feet
> Shall I myself be lying
>   when they range the screens around?
> And say shall I groan in dying,
>   as I twist the sweaty sheet?
> Or grasp for breath uncrying,
>   as I feel my senses drown'd
> While the air is swimming with insects
>   and children play in the street?

This naked fear lurks between the lines of Larkin's poem; it is the more profoundly chilling, for being understated. In comparison, Betjeman's anguish at the thought of leaving this world trembles on the edge of self-pity. His passionate love of the physical world is sensed in the description of a summer garden, in all its vibrant loveliness, which occurs at the beginning of the poem:

> Apple and plum espaliers
>   basked upon bricks of brown;
> The air was swimming with insects,
>   and children played in the street.

As he takes in this idyllic scene, he sees a housefly caught in a spider's web and describes the grisly spectacle minutely. Betjeman seems to identify himself, as Gray did, with the gaily insouciant fly which swings unawares, 'Slap into slithery rigging' and to whose 'fizzing, hopeless fight' with death the natural world is so indifferent. In the poem, he appears to be saying that we do not deserve what is coming to us. Larkin, on the other hand, says: deserve it or not, it's going to happen. It is a more dignified point of view, to say the least.

John Press, it must be said, has acquitted Betjeman of self-pity in this poem, believing that it heroically recognizes that 'the cycle of natural growth will continue, that, in every generation, children play on, unmindful of the suffering around them and that in the midst of death we are in life'. But this, it seems, says more than the poem for Betjeman appears to be crying at exclusion – as, of course, most of us will – rather than joyously accepting 'the cycle of natural growth'. The children's voices, the liquid air, are reminders of what he is losing, as indifferent to his fate as the 'inflexible nurses' feet' and conveying as little comfort in this final extremity. As Mr Press says: 'We are left to discern for ourselves the links between the sets of images, to respond to the poem's emotional development.' He might have added the words, 'in our own way'; which is perhaps a sign that the emotion is insufficiently realized, that the poet himself is not quite sure what he is saying.

In 'Inevitable', Betjeman returns to the subject of his father's death. Despite the sincerity of the feeling, there is, however, a certain slackness of diction: a charge which could not be levelled against 'The Cottage Hospital'. Lines such as, 'Although we knew his death was near, we fought against it hard' or 'Then came the time when he knew that he was through' have no bite and the image of the dying man looking 'like a cast-off Teddy bear' is weak; whatever its personal significance for such a well-known arctophile as Betjeman.

Betjeman felt guilty about his neglect of his father, his failure to repay his love while he was alive. He felt accused by the eyes which looked into his before the moment of death because it seemed his father's 'final generosity', one more debt he could not repay. This death-bed scene is referred to in another poem, 'A Child Ill', which is about his own son. It is an extremely sentimental poem; as, indeed, it could hardly fail to be. One imagines that it was written very close to the events with which it deals for it is more in the nature of a private prayer than a finished poem.

> My father looked at me and died
> Before my soul made full reply.
> Lord, leave this other Light alight –
> Oh, little body, do not die.

If depth of feeling were alone enough to make a good poem, this would be one of Betjeman's best. But it is our natural sympathy with a father's anxiety rather than the poem itself which gives it any power it has. The directness of the reiterated, 'Oh, little body, do not die' is impressive but we also experience a feeling of embarrassment, like people coming unexpectedly on a scene of private grief. In fact, such words, set down in cold print, seem merely banal and not the genuine coinage of grief; though, during moments of intense feeling, we often express ourselves in clichés.

Betjeman's sense of guilt is the subject of another poem, 'Remorse', which springs from memories of his mother's last illness. As with his father, Betjeman has a gnawing feeling that he did not give his mother – 'She whom I loved and left' – as much love as she deserved. There is, of course, a sense in which guilt is a self-indulgent emotion; though it is no less real and painful for that. In this poem, Betjeman says that to lose sight of his own 'neglect and unkindness', he 'would listen even again to that labouring breath'. This seems, on the face of it, an odd thing to say, suggesting that Betjeman would have his mother relive her suffering in order to expiate his own guilt. Its very ambiguity, not to say self-contradictoriness, reinforces the suspicion that Betjeman is inclined to savour remorse in the same way that others savour success. It satisfies the same need for self-abasement as his wilful prostration before those mountainous sports girls. Once again, comparison with Larkin is apposite. Larkin's 'Reference Back' is about his mother and the unequalness of their love. While Betjeman whips himself into a fury of guilt, Larkin accepts that we do not always love as well as we are loved and that we can never repair the loss, no matter how much we might regret it. Time deceives, lays a false scent by reminding us of what we once had and suggesting that, 'By acting differently we could have kept it so'. Betjeman, on the other hand, seems to believe that things might have been different; which is not at all the same thing as being saddened by the thought that they never could have been.

Betjeman, of course, is a demonstrative and emotional man. Such a nature, whilst capable of love and acts of unselfishness, is particularly prone to feelings of guilt and remorse. He is incapable of dispelling these feelings by the exercise of reason. A poem such as 'Remorse' fails not for want of sincerity but because self-pity is not amenable to translation into art; any more than the sort of raw anxiety occasioned by the present illness of a much-loved child. Although these poems are not entirely successful, they show

Betjeman expressing feelings which, though dealt with more
memorably elsewhere, would, at one time, have been completely
outside his range.

The topographical poems of these years, as has been said, are
more concerned with Betjeman's present discontents than with the
places themselves. In particular, they are suffused with nostalgia
and regret for the lost world of childhood. 'Harrow-on-the-Hill',
with its captivating music, its sensuous alliteration and
assonances, has its origin in memories of childhood holidays,
when the dull north London suburb near which he lived would be
transfigured by images of Cornwall: poplars whispering of the
sea; the railway sounding like 'the thunder of the rollers'; Harrow-
on-the-Hill itself like 'a rocky island', its burgess-filled churchyard
'full of sailors' graves'. But the expansive, untrammelled
imagination of the child which can thus transform humdrum
reality, endow common objects with magical significance, soon
fades. The final stanza is interrogatory, questioning the exulting
certainty of the child's confident vision and, by implication,
regretting that the vision has faded. The adult knows that there is
no secret glory to be glimpsed behind appearance's bland façade.

> There's a storm cloud to the westward over Kenton,
> There's a line of harbour lights at Perivale,
> Is it rounding rough Pentire in a flood of sunset fire
> The little fleet of trawlers under sail?
> Can those boats be only roof tops
> As they stream along the skyline
> In a race for port and Padstow
> With the gale?

In 'Hertfordshire', he recalls his father's disappointment at his
incompetence with a gun. The quiet rural county with its thatched
cottages and weather-boarded mills, has, since those days, suffered
a 'devastating change':

> One can't be sure where London ends,
> New towns have filled the fields of root
> Where father and his business friends
> Drove in the Landaulette to shoot . . .

A once known place has become 'ill and strange' and, though the
landscape once seemed 'unwelcome' to him, its despoliation brings

to mind memories of his father who would have minded this change far more than his son's 'mishandling of a gun'. This shared sense of loss brings him closer to his dead father for he is aware that, for all their differences at the time, they both belonged to that faded past. For the present, which has filled the county with 'brick boxes' which 'glitter in the sun', Betjeman feels no such affinity.

'Essex', too, turns on memories of childhood excursions with his father. The 'sweet, uneventful countryside' which he once knew is captured in the colour plates of an old guidebook. It is, of course, gone for ever; so completely that it now seems like a mirage. The departed beauties glimpsed in the colour plates as well as the archaic style of the captions which accompany them are faintly unreal, a hopeless romantic dream. Essex, in the guidebook's glamorizing mirror, takes on the appearance of an earthly paradise from which we are all now excluded. But the very lushness of the guidebook's picturesque style – 'The vagrant visitor erstwhile . . . Could wend by hedgerow-side and stile, /From Benfleet down to Leigh-on-Sea' – suggests such perfection only ever existed in the imagination. Betjeman's feeling of exclusion from 'that Edwardian "erstwhile" ', however, is not made any less painful when he compares the county as it is with the guidebook's Edwardian never-never-land. Now there is nothing left even for purple prose to embroider.

'Norfolk' is the best of these poems which recall the landscapes of childhood. It recalls holidays on the Norfolk Broads: the warmth and security of his cabin at night, the pleasure he then took in his father's company. But now 'These Norfolk lanes recall lost inno-cence', painfully making him aware of the gulf between what he then was and what he now is. In this poem, the landscape has not been desecrated; only knowledge has modified his response to its familiar features:

> The church is just the same, though now I know
> Fowler of Louth restored it.

It is the changes which have taken place within himself rather than those wrought on the place which distress him: 'How did the Devil come? When first attack?' The poem ends with a pathetically vain plea that 'the rapturous ignorance of long ago' might be restored:

> The peace, before the dreadful daylight starts,
> Of unkept promises and broken hearts.

The burden of guilt, the sense of failure, the gnawing anxiety which weigh down adulthood do not lead Betjeman into the belief that childhood is entirely innocent, that it has no terrors of its own. He is quite aware that the Devil claims his victims at an early age and in 'Original Sin on the Sussex Coast', the blank verse describes vicious bullying of the kind he had himself experienced. Cosy suburban domesticity is a sham, for the child as much as for the man:

> Does Mum, the Persil-user, still believe
> That there's no Devil and that youth is bliss?
> As certain as the sun behind the Downs
> And quite as plain to see, the Devil walks.

The 'dreadful daylight' does not so much bring the capacity to hurt and be hurt, for youth contains these in abundance; it is rather the sense of guilt, oppressive and stifling, which is the unique gift of maturity, as so many of these poems testify. Whilst, on occasion, Betjeman might be accused of wallowing in guilt, in a poem such as 'Greenaway' his night fears are set forth with dreadful clarity and a marked absence of self-pity. In his dreams, the stretch of coastline which he knows so well is transformed and he imagines himself dragged towards the 'dreadful jaws' of some sea-monster, a sort of Old Testament instrument of vengeance. In another poem, 'Pershore Station, *or* A Liverish Journey First Class', the ample movement of the verse, reflecting the poet's outward air of prosperous well-being, is at variance with the 'deadweight' of guilt and self-pity which afflicts him on account of his unfaithfulness and lack of consideration for his wife: 'With Guilt, Remorse, Eternity the void within me fills'.

If Betjeman's view of childhood is essentially unromantic, occasionally beamed with wonder but also shadowed with dark clouds, his Christianity, which is at the centre of many of these mature poems, is also far from cosy or merely complacent. His fine poem 'Christmas' begins descriptively and might seem set fair to develop into a conventional eulogy of the traditional Christmas being celebrated all over England: in remote villages; in provincial towns; in suburbs; even in London, even by the 'shining ones who dwell/Safe in the Dorchester Hotel'. But the season's real meaning is not contained in the yew boughs which deck the church; not in the paper decorations seen hanging in drab tenements; not in the hearty wishes of 'Merry Christmas to you all'; not in gifts or kind thoughts. Betjeman is undeceived by the bogus good feeling which abounds. He searches instead for the real meaning: 'And is it true?' he asks. 'And is it true, /This most tremendous tale of all.' He cannot answer the question he asks so urgently; like Hardy in 'The Oxen', he hopes it might be so. But while in Hardy's case, tactical hope merely deepens strategic pessimism, Betjeman's questioning is a desperate plea for reassurance. This elusive truth is the cornerstone of his existence. As he says elsewhere: 'For if the Christian's faith's untrue? /What is the point of me and you?' If the sacraments do not contain the whole meaning of life, nothing else can. He knows that the trappings of a Dingley Dell Christmas – gifts, carols, the 'love that in a family dwells' – ultimately are as nothing beside 'this single Truth' of which he can be only partially certain and which yet alone gives life a purpose and a meaning: 'That God was Man in Palestine /And lives to-day in Bread and Wine.'

Where previously Betjeman had made gentle fun of the Church – in poems such as 'Our Padre' or 'Exchange of Livings' – he has now gained the confidence to celebrate and affirm his deep love for it: its architecture and its ritual. He has no mystical vision which sees beyond these symbols and perceives God direct. They are the sheet anchor of his faith, such as it is. His religious speculations – 'Church of England thoughts' as he calls them – are occasioned by sights, sounds and smells. He perceives God through his senses. A church is, quite literally, God's house with God immanent, not only in the sacraments, but in box-pews, reredoses, sculptured capitals and stained glass. Church architecture is as expressive of God as the Surrey pines are of Miss Joan Hunter Dunn. In 'Sunday Morning, King's Cambridge', architecture and worship combine so that the chapel's roof can be said to be buttressed by prayer, the congregation to be singing not only with the choir but with the 'great crowned organ case' as it gathers 'to praise Eternity contained in Time and coloured glass'. The medieval chapel is not just a building, a mere shell for the enactment of worship, but participates in that worship and 'contains' God in its furnishings.

In the occasional verses written in 1952 in aid of the restoration of St Katharine's, Chiselhampton, Betjeman characteristically celebrates architectural details and their historical associations rather than the church's present significance within the community. For Betjeman, much of its meaning really lies in such things: the

chandeliers which hung when 'pre-Tractarian sermons roll'd', the
west gallery from which 'viol and serpent tooted out /The Tallis
tune to Ken'. Betjeman does not want the Church to change; its
value resides, for him, in its representation of continuity, stability,
order, beauty; qualities at a premium in the modern world.

Of all a church's usual trappings, the sound of its bells is the most
deeply affecting for Betjeman. Their varied sounds are the subject
of several poems. He has written that bells 'ring through our
literature, as they do over our meadows and roofs and few remaining
elms. Some may hate them for their melancholy, but they dislike
them chiefly, I think, because they are reminders of Eternity. In an
age of faith they were messengers of consolation.' In 'Wantage
Bells', they express Betjeman's gratitude for the 'reckless bestowing'
of the natural world. In another poem, 'Church of England
Thoughts', he writes exultantly of the sound of Magdalen Tower's
rich carillons:

> A multiplicity of bells,
>   A changing cadence, rich and deep,
> Swung from those pinnacles on high
> To fill the trees and flood the sky
>   And rock the sailing clouds to sleep.

Their sound brings to mind other bells of other churches: high ones
'blue with incense mist /Where reredoses twinkle gold'; humble
chapels of ease whose 'plaintive ting-tangs call /From many a gabled
western wall'; the numerous medieval 'country churches old and
pale' which are the glory of his life. Eternity may be heard in the
contending bells, but here their sound brings to mind comforting
ritual, peace and order rather than incalculable mysteries:

> A Church of England sound, it tells
>   Of 'moderate' worship, God and State,
> Where matins congregations go
> Conservative and good and slow
>   To elevations of the plate.

It is because it is 'Conservative and good and slow' that Betjeman
so loves 'our dear old C. of E.'. The six poems in *Poems in the Porch*
(1954), written originally for broadcast and later published by the
S.P.C.K., are loving celebrations of his Church. As he says, 'they
do not pretend to be poetry': though one of them, 'Diary of a

Church Mouse', has established itself in the canon, Philip Larkin even finding room for it in the *Oxford Book of Twentieth Century Verse*. It is not markedly better than the others, however, and its little joke about the church being filled 'With people I don't see at all / Except at Harvest Festival', as a sort of punchline at the end, is rather smug. The chief interest of the poems in this pamphlet is the light which they throw on the nature of Betjeman's religion, the very special place which the Church of England occupies in his affections: 'The kindest church to me on earth'. While there are some (thinking, perhaps, of Evelyn Waugh), 'who like things fully / Argued out, and call you "woolly" ', for Betjeman, there is 'refuge in the C. of E.'; though it is a refuge into which he cannot slip easily or naturally. He has hope rather than faith. Much as he craves 'the Grace most firmly to believe', doubt continues to oppress him and his worldliness to offer temptations of its own, rarely resisted and always regretted.

In these occasional verses, Betjeman specifically disclaims the intention of arguing theology or baring his own soul. His purpose is simply to give thanks, to celebrate a human institution in all its rich diversity – its churches, its hard-working vicars, its church-wardens, the ladies who arrange the flowers, even the humble church mouse – which is tolerant enough to welcome even so inveterate a backslider as himself. He finds things to censure, however, as well as to praise. He deplores the Children's Corners in cathedrals and the sort of genteel evasiveness which insists on the graveyard being renamed a Garden of Rest, equips it with a suburban bird-bath and adorns the headstone with saccharine phrases:

> Oh why do people waste their breath
> Inventing dainty names for death?
> On the old tombstones of the past
> We do not read 'At peace at last'
> But simply 'died' or plain 'departed'.
> It's no good being chicken-hearted.
> We die; that's that; our flesh decays
> Or disappears in other ways.

Betjeman's objection to this sort of 'ghastly good taste' is as much social as spiritual. He disapproves of 'At peace at last' for much the same reason as he winces at talk of doilies, fish-knives, cruets,

serviettes and all those other non-U words and phrases listed in that
snobbish and unfunny catalogue of incorrect usage, 'How to Get
On in Society': a poem which it is only fair to say that Betjeman has
himself disowned.

It is, in fact, the snobbery which informs so many of Betjeman's
attitudes and beliefs which is the major deterrent to a proper
appreciation of his writing. Beside the grand contempt for democracy and progress expressed by Yeats and Eliot, Betjeman seems to
be doing no more than fussing about what is considered to be good
form or the done thing; the violation of mere shibboleths. Rather
than expressing a sense of metaphysical outrage at the futility,
rootlessness and cultural dislocation of the century in which he lives
(as both Eliot and Yeats did) Betjeman seems merely nostalgic,
regretting the passing of an age in which there were fewer cars and
more servants. Bernard Bergonzi has said that Betjeman's satires
fail not because the poet is insufficiently full of hate but 'because he
has no very clear convictions from which to direct his attacks'. It is
true that, apart from a love for old buildings, a rather emotional
attachment to the Church of England and a nostalgic belief that life
was better in the prelapsarian world before 1914, Betjeman has no
very solid intellectual framework with which to support his attacks
on modern civilization. Bernard Bergonzi continues: 'It is one thing
to complain that,

> Mere anarchy is loosed upon the world,
> The blood-dimmed tide is loosed, and everywhere
> The ceremony of innocence is drowned

if one is writing with the aristocratic standards of a Yeats, and quite
another to make a similar complaint if one's own cultural heroes are
vulgarians like the Pooters.'

These are impressive charges and have some substance. Betjeman,
of course, does not regard the Pooters as vulgarians. He sees a
dignity in their simple lives as well as integrity, humour, individuality. Their belief in established values, thrift and respectability;
their genuine innocence, inspire his respect; particularly when he
contrasts it with the pseudo-sophistication of the present. In a poem
such as 'Middlesex', where the Pooters are used to point this
contrast, Betjeman is doing no more than register his conviction
that the Pooters were less standardized products than their present-
day counterparts who take their values from television and adver-

tisements. Living in an age of faith, they also had a greater sense of belonging, an awareness of being part of something greater than themselves. Despite Professor Bergonzi's peculiar belief that 'aristocratic standards' alone sanctify disdain, 'Middlesex' succeeds entirely on its own terms.

Professor Bergonzi's strictures carry more weight, however, when he turns his attention to overtly satirical poems where the faintness of Betjeman's convictions is often all too obvious. 'The Dear Old Village', though competent and full of adroit social observation, does not, in the end, add up to much. Nor, in fact, does its companion piece, 'The Village Inn'. These poems succeed as *vers de société* but fail as satire. In fact, when Betjeman attempts to draw conclusions from his observations, he fails: the satire seems no more than prejudice:

> An eight-hour day for all, and more than three
> Of these are occupied in making tea
> And talking over what we all agree –
> Though 'Music while you work' is now our wont
> It's not so nice as 'Music while you don't.'
> Squire, parson, schoolmaster turn in their graves.
> And *let* them turn. We are no longer slaves.

Philip Larkin has praised these lines as 'not only a pertinent summary of a subject no other present-day British poet has tried to deal with but singularly unforgettable'. The first part is, indeed, neat. It is the last two lines, however, in which Betjeman seems to suggest that things were better in the days of the old village hierarchy when people knew their place, which are at once weak and positively antipathetic. Why should Betjeman, who loves the leisured life of the country house, patronize the workers for their laziness? Is it not a case of the paradox which Roger Woddis exposes in his 'Ethics for Everyman': that while 'Workers are absentees, /Businessmen relax'? Betjeman is here saying nothing more admirable than that things were better when there was one law for the rich and one for the poor.

'Huxley Hall', with its rhythmical echoes of Tennyson's 'Locksley Hall', is one of Betjeman's least successful satires. One misses the acute social observation which is the redeeming feature of 'The Dear Old Village'. It is not even clear just what is being satirized; though one assumes it is the old bogy, Progress. The children are 'carefree'

and have 'released their inhibitions', an infallible sign that all is not
well in Betjeman's view; a bland rationalism, signalled by the name
Huxley, reigns over all. But the 'bright, hygienic hell' in which the
poet inexplicably finds himself is only a garden city café, a rather
odd starting-point for an all-out attack on the century's spiritual
bankruptcy; as odd as the bizarre vision of the woman, comfortably
untidy, 'dropping butter on her book', with which it is opposed.
Against this socially desirable, spiritually undesirable world, with
its puritan suggestions of health and efficiency, all Betjeman can
muster is 'a faint conviction that we may be born in Sin'. As with
'Group Life: Letchworth', one feels that a flimsy Aunt Sally has
been put up for no other purpose than to be knocked down – and
with weightless coconuts at that.

Betjeman's beliefs, though passionate and sincere, are too riddled
with doubt to form the basis for an attack on anything. It is his
fundamental lack of intellectual rigour which accounts for this; he
is a man of feeling rather than a thinker. As a writer of *vers de
société*, he is effective and penetrating. His direct satires, however,
succeed only when his target is a small one: municipal vandalism;
the insensitivities of big business; get-rich-quick farmers. This 'light
verse', so often praised and regarded as his typical product is, in
fact, the least successful part of his work. To see him as the natural
successor of writers such as Praed is greatly to misunderstand him.
Praed succeeds *only* when he is being funny; Betjeman succeeds
most often when he is being entirely serious. Betjeman, of course,
admires Praed for his consummate craftsmanship and metrical skill
and pays tribute to him in 'Winthrop Mackworth Redivivus', which
adapts the metre of 'Goodnight to the Season'. But is it only a
mildly amusing performance comparable to, say, 'Hunter Trials'.
For his real successes, one must look elsewhere.

This borrowing from Praed is a typical device. Betjeman loves to
set up echoes of other writers, which the reader may or may not
spot. His favourite quarries are minor nineteenth-century poets of
whose works one would need a knowledge as encyclopaedic as
Betjeman's to pick up all the references. Recognizing the old tune
to which the new song is set is the sort of parlour game which John
Sparrow enjoys playing in connection with Betjeman's work. But
Betjeman, like T. S. Eliot, would be seriously devalued if he were
seen as no more than a sophisticated *pasticheur*. It is always the new
song rather than the old tune which matters; though the relationship

between the two is often piquant. There can be no doubt, however, that, for all his borrowings, Betjeman has succeeded in creating an original and distinctive tone of voice, an individual style. A deep knowledge of the more recondite nineteenth-century poets is no more essential to an understanding of his verse than, say, a working knowledge of Chapman's *Handbook of Birds of Eastern North America* is to an understanding of *The Waste Land*.

Betjeman's models are certainly unusual ones. He has said, for instance, how much he enjoys the 'emphatic obviousness and musical simplicity' of Longfellow's verse. It would not be surprising if he liked Mahony's over-rhymed, over-familiar 'Bells of Shandon'. His fondness for Longfellow is seen in two poems which parody that poet's sledge-hammer trochees and regularly placed caesuras: 'Longfellow's Visit to Venice' and 'A Literary Discovery'. The latter originated, like 'How to Get On in Society', as a set-piece for *Time and Tide*; it is embedded in a portentous *apparatus criticus* and purports to be the discovery of a manuscript poem by Henry Wood, husband of the Victorian novelist, in celebration of a supposed visit by Longfellow to the Woods' house, Gomshall Towers in Surrey.

> To the greeting of his hostess answered Mr Longfellow:
> 'Ma'am, your fine historic mansion is a dream of mine come
>   true.
> 'Tis, amid its pines and hemlocks, some Helvetian rendezvous.'

A footnote explains solemnly: 'The poet must be in error. There is no *old* mansion at Gomshall. But he may have thought Gomshall Towers old because of the crenellations, and historic because of its hostess.' It is an entertaining *jeu d'esprit*.

Not all the allusions are to obscure or minor poets, however. 'The Licorice Fields at Pontefract' refers ironically to Yeats's familiar lyric, 'Down by the salley gardens my love and I did meet'.

> In the licorice fields at Pontefract
>   My love and I did meet
> And many a burdened licorice bush
>   Was blooming round our feet . . .

It is one of Betjeman's best 'amatory' poems, combining absurdity and passion to delightful effect:

> She cast her blazing eyes on me
>   And plucked a licorice leaf;
> I was her captive slave and she
>   My red-haired robber chief.
> Oh love! for love I could not speak,
> It left me winded, wilting, weak
> And held in brown arms strong and bare
> And wound with flaming ropes of hair.

As in earlier poems of the same type, Betjeman is here the weak, adoring male enthralled by the strapping Amazon; though, at least, on this occasion he finds fulfilment of a sort. In 'The Olympic Girl' he is back in his more familiar role of pathetic and despised devotee of the huge sports girl, afraid to take lust to its obvious and devastating conclusion.

> Fair tigress of the tennis courts,
> So short in sleeve and strong in shorts,
> Little, alas, to you I mean,
> For I am bald and old and green.

These poems are passionate and sensual for all their perversity; they express a sort of impure pleasure in the delights of the flesh, though it is a pleasure which, more often than not, is clouded by feelings of inferiority and guilt. The poems, however, are joyful even when admiration does not lead to consummation.

The mood changes dramatically in two powerful poems which show a new side of Betjeman: 'Sun and Fun' and 'Late Flowering Lust'. These poems both vividly describe how the physical repulsiveness of age does nothing to diminish the persistent, if unseemly, desire for love. The elderly night-club proprietress in 'Sun and Fun' is a tragic figure, a survival of the gay twenties washed up in an age she does not understand. She is treated more sympathetically than Mews Flat Mona or D'Arcy Honeybunn in William Plomer's cruel and savage poems, though Plomer is a poet often compared with Betjeman. It is the pathos rather than the grotesquerie which Betjeman records and, despite the light verse rhythms, fear strikes home:

> But I'm dying now and done for,
> What on earth was all the fun for?
>   For I'm old and ill and terrified and tight.

In 'Late Flowering Lust', the two ageing bodies embracing are turned into two skeletons holding each other tight, a sort of *danse macabre*:

> Dark sockets look on emptiness
> Which once was loving-eyed,
> The mouth that opens for a kiss
> Has got no tongue inside.

Now that he is older and with death drawing ever nearer and the body's decay all too apparent, he has lost 'the joys I had /When I was young in sin'. It is fear rather than lust which inflames the aged lovers:

> Too long we let our bodies cling,
> We cannot hide disgust
> At all the thoughts that in us spring
> From this late-flowering lust.

Such a poem should have dispelled the myth that Betjeman was merely an entertainer. *A Few Late Chrysanthemums*, in fact, contains little for our comfort. During these years, Betjeman struck a rich vein of poetic ore which he has only occasionally rediscovered since. The best poems of these years are not just the high-water mark of Betjeman's own achievement: they are some of the best poems written in English since the war.

CHAPTER FIVE

BLANK VERSIFIER

Summoned by Bells, Betjeman's blank-verse autobiography, is divided into nine sections which trace the poet's development from early childhood in Highgate and Cornwall, through the horrors of private and public schools, to his final emergence as a fully realized human being at Oxford in the twenties. It had been extensively presented in pre-publication extracts before its formal appearance, just in time for the Christmas trade, late in 1960. His publishers, hardly surprisingly, expected it to do well, for *Collected Poems* had already sold something like one hundred thousand copies. They optimistically suggested that this autobiographical fragment would have a sequel; though this particular hope has so far remained unfulfilled. The large blind-stamped boards; the decorated end-papers; the thick antique laid paper; the archaic typeface; the illustrations (particularly hideous and child-like); the quaint, old-fashioned practice of providing synopses at the beginning of each chapter, conspired to give the book the air of being a deliberately made artefact designed for presentation to Aunt Daisy.

Its reception was predictably mixed. Many critics threw up their hands in horror at what they dismissed as a self-indulgent wallow in nostalgia of the most sentimental kind executed in the blankest of blank verse. Though Philip Larkin welcomed its appearance in a brilliant and highly laudatory review in the *Spectator*, John Wain savaged it in the *Observer* whilst Frank Kermode (bizarrely yoking Henry Miller and Betjeman together for the purpose of his article) confessed himself disappointed, in a piece published in *Encounter*. Betjeman, evidently forgetting Larkin, once remarked that he 'always had filthy reviews for it', adding that he 'didn't think it very good' himself.

The very idea of writing an autobiography in blank verse seems, in the latter half of the twentieth century, an act of self-indulgence and wilful eccentricity which positively courts ridicule. Betjeman did not help matters by saying that he had been reading *The Prelude* and Tennyson's English idylls before deciding to give 'some moments in the sheltered life of a middle-class youth' a similar treatment for, needless to say, he falls short of his august models. He has said more than once that he finds it easier to write blank verse than prose and, in the prefatory note to the poem, (written in the third person), he says that he 'has gone as near prose as he dare' and that he 'chose blank verse, for all but the more hilarious moments, because he found it best suited to brevity and the rapid changes of mood and subject'. None of this, it must be said, sounds very convincing as an explanation for what remains an obstinately eccentric enterprise. Although Betjeman, on the whole, manages to justify his choice of medium, one is sometimes reminded of Eliot's observation to the effect that anything which can be said as well in prose can be said better in prose. Betjeman's very facility occasionally produces dull patches; though wry humour and delicate irony generally succeed in lifting the tone of the verse above the level of banality. What Frank Kermode has called 'the wanton particularity' of Betjeman's habitual references to material objects (Betjeman seems to remember the name of everything from the kind of toothpaste which he used to the name of the stuff which was used to paint the garden fence) as well as the almost total recall which enables him to present sights, sounds and smells of furthest childhood as if they belonged to yesterday, give the writing sharpness of outline, an almost pictorial clarity, which would be beyond the powers of a mere facile peddler in nostalgia for an imagined paradise lost.

Betjeman had already shown his paces as a blank versifier in a poem called 'Sunday Afternoon Service in St Enodoc Church, Cornwall' from *New Bats in Old Belfries*. In retrospect, this seems to have been a sort of dress rehearsal for the Cornish chapter of *Summoned by Bells*. It is a fine piece of writing and the magnificent concluding description of the sea remains one of his most brilliant effects:

Forced by the backwash, see the nearest wave
Rise to a wall of huge, translucent green
And crumble into spray along the top
Blown seaward by the land-breeze. Now she breaks
And in an arch of thunder plunges down
To burst and tumble, foam on top of foam,
Criss-crossing, baffled, sucked and shot again,
A waterfall of whiteness, down a rock,
Without a source but roller's furthest reach:
And tufts of sea-pink, high and dry for years,
Are flooded out of ledges, boulders seem
No bigger than a pebble washed about
In this tremendous tide.

There is nothing flaccid or dull about this and a note of dramatic
urgency, maintained throughout, ensures that the poem never flags,
as *Summoned by Bells* occasionally does. The blank verse line is
supple and muscular; there are no gratuitous grace notes put in only
to sustain the rhythm of the five-beat line. We are aware that the
scene which is being described is a real place rather than some
imaginary coastline with pasteboard cliffs and painted ocean, with
the result that words and images carry their full weight of meaning;
they are not simply tokens manipulated by an accomplished craftsman.

Summoned by Bells rarely reaches such heights; though there are
passages of precise description, in which one feels that the natural
world is being observed as if under a magnifying glass, which are
very remarkable in their own way.

Sometimes, thank God, they left me all alone
In our small patch of garden in the front,
With clinker rockery and London Pride
And barren lawn and lumps of yellow clay
As mouldable as smelly Plasticine.
I used to turn the heavy stones to watch
The shiny red and waiting centipede
Which darted out of sight: the woodlouse slow
And flat; the other greyish-bluey kind
Which rolled into a ball till I was gone
Out of the gate to venture down the hill.

There is an almost hallucinatory quality in this digging up of images, so precise and clear, from childhood's deepest recesses. The picture it creates is reminiscent of Richard Dadd's painting, *The Fairy Feller's Masterstroke*, in which a patch of ground is presented in similarly magical close-up. This impassioned receptivity to sensual experience is the distinguishing feature of the best writing in *Summoned by Bells*. As Betjeman says, if adult life is measured out in coffee spoons: 'Childhood is measured out by sounds and smells /And sights, before the dark of reason grows.'

One of the reasons why *Summoned by Bells* is not continuously satisfying is that too many of the incidents are already familiar from earlier poems. One thinks, for instance, of 'Original Sin on the Sussex Coast', about childhood bullying, and 'False Security', which turns on a story which is recounted (in slightly different form) in the longer poem. Similarly, childhood impressions of Cornwall and Highgate have provided the background for many poems which are not improved on here. If one compares, for instance, 'N.W.5 & N.6' which recalls the sadistic nurse who was responsible for the dawn of guilt in her young charge, with the parallel passage in *Summoned by Bells*, one sees that there has been a loss both in concentration of language and in emotional authority. Having definitively treated this subject in one of his best poems, Betjeman's return to the subject later seems an act of supererogation.

> I see black oak twigs outlined on the sky,
> Red squirrels on the Burdett-Coutts estate.
> I ask my nurse the question 'Will I die?'
> As bells from sad St Anne's ring out so late,
> 'And if I do die, will I go to Heaven?'
> Highgate at eventide. Nineteen-eleven.
>
> 'You will. I won't.' From that cheap nursery-maid,
> Sadist and puritan as now I see,
> I first learned what it was to be afraid,
> Forcibly fed when sprawled across her knee
> Lock'd into cupboards, left alone all day,
> 'World without end.' What fearsome words to pray.
>
> 'World without end'. It was not what she'ld do
> That frightened me so much as did her fear

And guilt at endlessness. I caught them too,
Hating to think of sphere succeeding sphere
Into eternity and God's dread will.
I caught her terror then. I have it still.

This is far better than anything in *Summoned by Bells* and it may well
have been this sense of *déjà vu* combined with failure to achieve the
intensity of the first rendering of the experience which accounted
for some critics' preference for the book's concluding section, 'The
Opening World', which describes his time at Oxford, a period in
his life which Betjeman had not written about before.

But though this section is interesting for the amount of autobiographical information it provides, the appearance of so many
familiar names, the routine awarding of neat compliments to old
friends very soon becomes dull. In fact, it contains some of the least
memorable writing in the whole poem, even if one does not accept
Frank Kermode's judgement that the long 'irregular ode' which
brings it to a close is better than the blank verse which surrounds it.
It is the descriptive passages in the early sections, despite the
familiarity of locales and incidents, which stay in the mind: the
sharp, clear recollection of days at his father's factory or mornings
on the beach in Cornwall.

Nose! Smell again the early morning smells:
Congealing bacon and my father's pipe;
The after-breakfast freshness out of doors
Where sun had dried the heavy dew and freed
Acres of thyme to scent the links and lawns;
The rotten apples on our shady path
Where blowflies settled upon squashy heaps,
Intent and gorging; at the garden gate
Reek of Solignum on the wooden fence;
Mint round the spring, and fennel in the lane,
And honeysuckle wafted from the hedge;
The Lynams' cess-pool like a body-blow;
Then, clean, medicinal and cold – the sea.

As description this could not be bettered; there is nothing vague or
misty about it. Whilst the names of herbs and plants, the brand-
name of the preservative used for the fence, the name of the family
who owned the noisome cess-pool, may have meant little to a child,

their presence gives the memory its authenticity and resonance. Although it is the sense of smell which is being evoked one gets, too, the impression of a summer's day: its airy lightness, its sense of everything being thrown into high relief, an effect intensified by the proximity of the sea. The selection and presentation of detail produces an effect of remarkable verisimilitude so that the only possible critical response is the simple one: 'Yes, that is what it must have been like.' As the impulse behind the passage is nothing more than the wish to preserve and share an experience, such a response shows that Betjeman has achieved his object. Impassioned description of this kind, while not the best thing which poetry is capable of, is, nevertheless, impossible not to admire when managed so well.

As Philip Larkin observed in his review, *Summoned by Bells* is not really about Betjeman at all for he is not an egoist but rather 'that rare thing, an extrovert sensitive, not interested in himself but in the experiences which being himself enables him to savour, including that of being himself'. This is a remarkably perceptive judgement. It is his openness to experience, his sensitivity to place and atmosphere, his capacity for sheer wonder and delight, as well, of course, as his skill in transforming his perceptions into art which accounts for most of the pleasure which the book gives. Because he is not interested in mapping out the chronology of his life but rather in presenting sensory experience, the choice of verse as the medium for his autobiography is a credible, if unusual, one. What merely happens to happen – 'the hail of occurrence', as Larkin calls it, is as nothing to the opportunity for sensual delight which life affords. It is the impulse to preserve what he sees and feels which Betjeman has said made him determined to be a poet and it is, as Larkin suggests, Betjeman the extrovert sensitive, impassioned and observant, rather than Betjeman the thinker or the doer who emerges from these recollections. One learns relatively little about what actually goes on inside him and relatively little about what he actually does, though there is an amount of self-revelation (as there is, to a much greater extent, in the shorter poems); but, undeniably one sees, hears and smells the things he saw, heard and smelt. It is as a recorder and sharer of experience rather than as an active protagonist that Betjeman comes across in the book. This might have been more difficult to achieve had he chosen to write his autobiography in prose as, for one thing, the ego would, inevitably, have had a much larger canvas on which to spread itself.

Summoned by Bells is, undeniably, one of those works of literature which can only be properly understood and properly appreciated if one is prepared to accept that the provision of pleasure is a legitimate goal for a writer. The book fulfils the pleasure-principle even when what is being described is not particularly pleasurable, for it is evident throughout that Betjeman, however many disappointments and humiliations he has suffered, has derived immense delight from the experience of living. The pleasure which the book affords the reader is not the sort provided by great art. It is decorative rather than fundamentally enlightening. But although it may not leave one a different person after having read it, its best passages genuinely enrich and enhance life in the incidental way that only minor art can.

Nevertheless, despite its many delights, it would be an indulgent reader who did not succumb to occasional fatigue, either because of the sense of *déjà vu* or from boredom with a medium which tends inevitably towards monotony. As well as simply getting the facts across, the blank verse has to accommodate many shifts of mood and subject: from anecdote to impassioned description and back again. On the whole, these transitions are well managed rather than disconcerting and serve to demonstrate Betjeman's skill in a medium virtually ignored by other modern poets. But facility itself can, if extended too far, become boring. Betjeman tries, not altogether successfully, to overcome this particular kind of *ennui* by interpolating rhymed sections, in the manner of Tennyson's *The Princess*, which are intended to diversify the tone. These poems-within-a-poem, while providing a necessary variation in metre, are not in themselves sufficiently distinguished to be of real value in this respect. In fact, they fall considerably short of the best passages in the blank verse which frames them.

Part of the pleasure – though it is a very secondary one – must derive from the reader's awareness of the strangeness of the enterprise. It gives one something of a *frisson* to have the febrile world of Oxford in the twenties described in a form which the Victorians reserved for ponderous and moralizing epics which now lie unread and gathering dust on the shelves of old libraries. This presentation of the modern world in the forms of a traditional poetic technique is, of course, the hallmark of all Betjeman's writing and one might almost say that an enterprising literary tipster could have opened a book on the chances of Betjeman, should he ever decide to undertake an autobiography, choosing to write it in blank verse. But what is piquant and refreshing in a short lyrical poem is rather irritating in a work of the length of *Summoned by Bells*; only so much new wine can be poured into an old bottle.

There is, furthermore, a distressing triteness in some of the writing. As Frank Kermode pointed out, a line such as 'Deeply I loved thee, 31 West Hill!', which occurs early in the poem, 'would not be a tolerable line in a local newspaper poet'. Its frightful banality is to some extent excused by the excellence of the writing which follows it, in which the things he loved about his childhood home are described. It nevertheless remains as irrefutable evidence of how badly Betjeman can sometimes write without even, apparently, being aware of it. Philip Larkin put the matter more tentatively and politely than Professor Kermode: 'How, without embarrassing us, can he write:

> Poor mother, walking bravely on the lawn,
> Her body one huge toothache! Would she die?
> And if she died could I forgive myself?'

The answer must surely be that he cannot. One passes over such lines because one believes them to be untypical. Larkin suggests, plausibly enough, that Betjeman's sincerity – 'as unselfconscious as it is absolute' – may in part explain the reader's leniency, but one has to guard against using this to excuse any descent into bathos. Poverty of language as well as catchpenny sentiment pulls one up short in this particular passage. 'Her body one huge toothache!' suggests an irony belied by the swift follow-on, 'Would she die?' Betjeman's feelings of guilt have been the subject of other poems which have not seemed bathetic; here it is not the sentiment but the language in which it is expressed which accounts for our feeling of embarrassment. Perhaps there are rather too many such passages in *Summoned by Bells* for it to be accounted an unqualified success by anybody.

In spite of the many pleasures and the instrinsic interest of the information which the poem conveys about Betjeman – information which would not be available from any other source – it is, perhaps, fortunate that there has been no sequel. 'Cricket Master' from *High and Low*, a sort of coda now included in reprints of *Summoned by Bells*, was presumably intended to form the first chapter of this sequel. It shows, however, that it would have been difficult to achieve the distinction of those fine descriptive passages which are the glory of the book, once all that was left was the occasional anecdote to be polished up and presented in verse form. 'Cricket Master', which does no more than that, indicates that the whole enterprise might have degenerated into absurdity if it had been extended any further. As Betjeman himself has said: 'I think people's lives are interesting only up until they're twenty-one. As soon as you get into life you meet people that you've heard of.' As it is, *Summoned by Bells* remains an interesting fragment which, despite the excellence of many of its best passages, cannot be regarded as entirely successful. One is certainly grateful that Betjeman decided to write it; but that does not prevent one from agreeing with John Press's verdict that it is 'not a volume one would recommend to anybody unacquainted with the author's shorter poems'.

CHAPTER SIX

SHADES OF EVENING

Betjeman's two most recent collections of verse – *High and Low* (1966) and *A Nip in the Air* (1974) – contain fewer good poems than any of the previous volumes. In his admirable anthology, *The Best of Betjeman*, John Guest includes only seven poems from these two books, and Philip Larkin includes not a single one in his otherwise very wide-ranging selection from Betjeman in *The Oxford Book of Twentieth Century Verse*. Although there are some good poems in both books, none achieves the high standard set by the best poems of his mature middle period, the decade between the appearance of *Selected Poems* (1948) and *Collected Poems* (1958). Instead of passion and deep feeling, there is accomplishment, serene craftsmanship, competence. As we read these poems, we cannot fail to be aware that most of the themes touched upon have been dealt with more memorably elsewhere. The reader's pleasure is tinged with regret for the time when Betjeman seemed incapable of producing a dull poem. Though the failures are less spectacular – there is nothing as bad as, say, 'Huxley Hall' or 'The Planster's Vision' – one is aware that competence has brought with it, all too often, a certain blandness and monotonous evenness of tone. This is particularly true of the topographical poems, hardly any of which hold up against such as 'Henley-on-Thames', 'Youth and Age', 'Parliament Hill Fields' and 'Ireland with Emily' from the forties, the period at which Betjeman's 'topophilia' was most intense.

High and Low begins with a series of 'landscapes' which illustrate this decline. The group of five Cornish scenes, following one after the other, produce an effect of sameness which diminishes their

individual impact. Their blandness is apparent in 'Cornish Cliffs',
a piece of pure description which dwells lovingly on the colours,
sounds and smells of the piece of Cornish coast which Betjeman
loves so well and has written about so often. It is a suavely
accomplished piece of work but there is an almost mechanical
slickness in the deft shuffling of images, an anodyne smoothness in
the versification, a certain lack of savour in the language:

> Nut-smell of gorse and honey-smell of ling
> Waft out to sea the freshness of the spring
> On sunny shallows, green and whispering.
>
> The wideness which the lark-song gives the sky
> Shrinks at the clang of sea-birds sailing by
> Whose notes are tuned to days when seas are high.

The same level tone and lack of intensity characterizes 'A Bay in
Anglesey', as they do most of the descriptive verse in *A Nip in the
Air*. The one surprising exception is a poem about Greece, the only
non-British landscape Betjeman has written about, called 'Greek
Orthodox'. This poem observes the landscape painted by his
beloved Lear – and also by his friend, Osbert Lancaster – with the
same enraptured eye which is used to dwell on English and Irish
scenes:

> Edward Lear,
> Show me the Greece of wrinkled olive boughs
> Above red earth; thin goats, instead of cows,
> Each with its bell; the shallow terraced soil;
> The stone-built wayside shrine; the yellow oil;
> The tiled and cross-shaped church, who knows how old
> Its ashlar walls of honey-coloured gold?
> Three centuries or ten? Of course, there'll be
> The long meander off to find the key.

There would seem to be a joke against himself concealed in this, for
it is certainly as odd to find Betjeman, of all people, who has
tottered off to find the keys of so many English parish churches
doing the same in Greece, as it is to find the church-bibber more
used to wondering if a church was 'restored with a vengeance about
eighteen-eighty-eight', unable to date a building within a span of
seven centuries. Piquant too, is the celebration of the ancient Greek

Orthodox church, sailing 'serenely over controversial tides', in terms more usually kept for his own 'dear old C. of E.'. Perhaps the unspoilt rural landscape of mainland Greece, its unprogressive and traditional church, seem now to have those qualities which he realizes have disappeared from England for ever.

'Winter Seascape', another of those poems which make up the opening section of *High and Low*, has the poet beholding 'a huge consoling sea'. Though the mood is different, one is irresistibly reminded of 'Greenaway', whose metre and rhyme scheme it exactly reproduces, so that stanzas from each of the poems could be transposed without upsetting the movement of the verse in the slightest. This sense of *déjà vu*, together with a certain lifelessness in the diction – to be seen in the cliché 'a mongrel hound gives tongue' which is there for no other reason than to sustain the rhyme – makes one fear that an authentic talent is in danger of being undermined by an excess of mere facility.

> Unheard, a mongrel hound gives tongue,
>   Unheard are shouts of little boys:
> What chance has any inland lung
>   Against this multi-water noise?

'Tregardock', often regarded as the best of these Cornish poems, if not the best poem in the whole collection, is certainly of a higher standard than any of its companions. But, though the language is more vigorous (there is nothing as limp as 'multi-water', which rather suggests an automatic washing machine), there are some disturbing false notes. The sudden upward swing in the verse, for instance, created by the internal rhyming of 'The grass bends down, the bracken's brown' is jarring in what is a sombre and melancholy poem, and the likening of the cliffs' 'waiting awfulness' to 'journalism full of hate' is weak; too personal and insufficiently concrete; though it is given a certain logical coherence within the poem by the final stanza, which explains why the image suggested itself:

> And I on my volcano edge
>   Exposed to ridicule and hate
> Still do not dare to leap the ledge
>   And smash to pieces on the slate.

This is a powerful and moving conclusion; though anyone who considered that it revealed Betjeman in a new or unexpected light should look again at some of the poems in *A Few Late Chrysanthemums*.

The mood of 'By the Ninth Green, St Enodoc' is less grim. The poem enshrines the sudden illumination of a particular moment. The metre derives from Campbell's 'Hohenlinden'. There is a questioning energy and power in its search for the meaning of this sudden stab of emotion, occasioned by a moment when he feels earth and sea and air suddenly cry out together, which is refreshing beside the vacuity of poems such as 'Cornish Cliffs' or 'Winter Seascape'; poems which resemble nothing so much as neat lengths of poetic ectoplasm.

> Why is it that a sunlit second sticks?
> What force collects all this and seeks to fix
> This fourth March morning nineteen sixty-six
>   Deep in my head?

'Old Friends' mingles familiar Cornish sights with memories of dead friends with whom the poet once shared this place:

> The tide is high and a sleepy Atlantic sends
>   Exploring ripple on ripple down Polzeath shore,
> And the gathering dark is full of the thought of friends
>   I shall see no more.

In the evening, the 'host of stars' suggests 'a host of souls' as he stops his car and looks up at the sky. He cannot bear the thought that his friends have simply ceased to be. He seeks reassurance that their spirits have somehow survived, that they are now 'one with the Celtic saints and the years between', that they, too, 'see the moonlit pools where ribbonweed drifts'. Such reassurance, though it is not quite certain how, seems to have been vouchsafed, for the poem ends in hope and certainty:

> As I reach our hill, I am part of a sea unseen –
>   The oppression lifts.

As well as these on the whole rather disappointing Cornish poems, there are three Irish poems which, though none of them measures up to 'Ireland with Emily', have qualities of their own which are not to be despised. 'A Lament for Moira McCavendish' is wonderfully melodic; smooth and sensuous like Moira herself. It actually improves on the sentimental ballads, in this respect, from which it so obviously derives. That oft-remarked poetic entity, 'the singing line', is nowhere so evident in the whole body of twentieth-century poetry. The exulting passion at the beginning and the hopeless desolation at the close of the journey to Moira carry conviction despite the seemingly parodic quaintness of the language ('O vein of my heart!'). Betjeman here, as elsewhere, works so naturally in an old convention that he seems to have absorbed his influences by a sort of poetic osmosis. He inhabits rather than parodies the style of the sentimental song and ballad writers with the result that Tom Moore himself would not have been sorry to own such a poem.

> Och Moira McCavendish! the fangs of the creeper
>   Have struck at the thatch and thrust open the door;
> The couch in the garden grows ranker and deeper
>   Than musk and potato which bloomed there before.
>
> Flow on, you remorseless and salmon-full waters!
>   What care I for prospects so silvery fair?
> The heart in me's dead, like your sweetest of daughters,
>   And I would that my spirit were lost on the air.

If this were no more than a tongue-in-cheek exercise in technique we would not be so moved. The very passion which underlies the poem lifts it above parody and has led Christopher Booker to conclude, rather exaggeratedly perhaps, that there is no more heartrending poem in the language.

'The Small Towns of Ireland' also shows Betjeman working naturally and freely in an alien convention: the patriotic, balladic style of the Irish 'hedge poets' whose works he has seen pinned up in pubs and general stores in that 'sad, beautiful country'. Betjeman manages to convey the mixture of passion and pride, the deep feeling for Mother Ireland which animates these unsophisticated but metrically adroit folk poets with whom he would seem to have so little in common. It is an Irishman's view of Ireland which counterpoints the haughty Anglo-Irish contempt for 'the last of Europe's stone age race' in 'Ireland with Emily'.

> I see thy grey granite, O grim House of Sessions!
>   I think of the judges who sat there in state
> And my mind travels back to our monster processions
>   To honour the heroes of brave Ninety-Eight.

> The barracks are burned where the Redcoats oppressed us,
>   The gaol is broke open, our people are free.
> Though Cromwell once cursed us, Saint Patrick has
>   blessed us –
>   The merciless English have fled o'er the sea.

Irish poetry has always meant a lot to Betjeman; as much as the Irish landscape or Irish architecture. He relishes the musical quality of so much of the verse, its delight in rhythm and rhyme for their own sake; its joy in the suggestive rather than the denotive power of language. It is just this sensuous and pure quality which he finds in the work of Tom Moore – 'Dear bard of my boyhood, mellifluous Moore' – to whom he pays tribute in 'Ireland's Own *or* The Burial of Thomas Moore'. The rhythms of Moore's work – compare, for instance, 'Pershore Station' with Moore's lyric 'At the mid hour of the night, when stars are weeping, I fly' – ripple through Betjeman's poems more frequently than those of any other single poet with the exception, perhaps, of Tennyson. And there are echoes of other Irish poets too: compare, for instance, Milliken's 'The Groves of Blarney' with 'An Impoverished Irish Peer'.

As well as poems about such familiar, not to say habitual, locations as Ireland and Cornwall, there are poems in *High and Low* on places which he has not written about before. Perhaps because his feeling for these places is less profound and his acquaintance with them may only extend to a single visit, these poems, for the most part, are rather inconsequential. 'An Edwardian Sunday, Broomhill, Sheffield' has the deftly executed lifelessness of a painting done from a photograph rather than from nature. It is a costume-piece: poignant, accomplished, pleasing but scarcely rising above the level of, say, the verse commentary which accompanied his documentary, *Metro-land*.

> By tramway excursion
> To Dore and to Totley
> In search of diversion
> The millworkers come;
> But in our arboreta
> The sounds are discreeter
> Of shoes upon stone –
> The worshippers wending
> To welcoming chapel,

Companioned or lone;
And over a pew there
See loveliness lean,
As Eve shows her apple
Through rich bombazine:
What love is born new there
In blushing eighteen!

These lines conjure up a particular time and a particular place but their niceness of phrasing and picturesque evocativeness is no substitute for the intimately remembered detail of, say, 'Parliament Hill Fields' or the energy and *brio* of 'Henley-on-Thames'. In fact, there is a slight whiff of the property basket about the poem.

The best of these poems about unfamiliar northern settings is 'Matlock Bath', the over-grown village and, in Betjeman's words, 'non-conformist spa' in Derbyshire; far less grand and metropolitan than its rivals such as Cheltenham or Harrogate, and nestling in the shadow of huge limestone crags which seem about to crash down on it. The precise imagery (the sound of hymns is described as being as 'sweet as strawberry jam'), the elegant phrasing, the skilful 'cutting' of Biblical texts and hymn titles, the consciously archaic use of capital letters for place names: all combine to pleasing effect making it a good, if not a great poem. As Betjeman traverses the slippery, vertiginous paths which thread the Heights of Abraham above the little spa, he is once again on his volcano's edge; though here the rather sinister non-conformist setting, the threat contained in the beetling cliffs which seem poised to break like a wave over the town (melting away 'The hardest Blue John ash-trays . . . in thermal steam') brings to mind thoughts of God's vengeance rather than of suicide.

Perhaps it's this that makes me shiver
As I ascend the slippery path
High, high above the sliding river
And terraces of Matlock Bath:
A sense of doom, a dread to see
The *Rock of Ages cleft for me*.

Such images of general destruction, forcing the return to a primal state of nature, fascinate Betjeman. One thinks, for instance, of the exhortation to the bombs in 'Slough' or the final image of the sea in

'Beside the Seaside'. In 'Delectable Duchy', from *A Nip in the Air*, he returns to this theme. The poem begins with a description of Cornwall as she now is against which Betjeman, typically, sets up the unspoilt Cornwall he remembers from his own childhood:

> The many-coloured cara's fill
> The salty marsh to Shilla Mill.
> And, foreground to the hanging wood,
> Are toilets where the cattle stood.
> The mint and meadowsweet would scent
> The brambly lane by which we went;
> Now, as we near the ocean roar,
> A smell of deep-fry haunts the shore.
> In pools beyond the reach of tides
> The Senior Service carton glides,
> And on the sand the surf-line lisps
> With wrappings of potato crisps.

As if to banish the horrible vision of a once beautiful landscape now irretrievably ruined, Betjeman imagines a great tidal wave breaking over it all, himself included, and leaving, in an image of great beauty and peace, a waste of water in which only the high points on Bodmin are visible:

> in windy criss-cross motion
> A waste of undulating ocean
> With, jutting out, a second Scilly,
> The isles of Roughtor and Brown Willy.

The twentieth century's tendency to destroy beauty wherever it is to be found, festooning it with litter or covering it with concrete, whips Betjeman into the same passionate fury it always did.

'Harvest Hymn' is the most famous, though by no means the best, of these satirical poems. It impishly adapts 'We plough the fields and scatter' to the creed of today's rich and insensitive farmer.

> We spray the fields and scatter
>   The poison on the ground
> So that no wicked wild flowers
>   Upon our farm be found.
> We like whatever helps us
>   To line our purse with pence;

The twenty-four-hour broiler-house
And neat electric fence.

Such use of hymn metres is, of course, a characteristic device. One thinks, for instance, of the gaily ironic lines dedicated to Martyn Skinner – an exact contemporary of Betjeman's, a poet, farmer and eccentric who left Oxfordshire in 1961 because it had become too noisy – which echo another familiar piece from *Hymns Ancient and Modern*, 'Stand up, Stand up for Jesus':

> Return, return to Ealing,
>   Worn poet of the farm!
> Regain your boyhood feeling
>   Of uninvaded calm!

'Inexpensive Progress' is one of Betjeman's most savage poems, full of the same contempt as 'Love is Dead', his famous prose commination on the subject of the average man. The present – 'O age without a soul' – is apostrophized thus:

> When all our roads are lighted
> By concrete monsters sited
>   Like gallows overhead,
> Bathed in the yellow vomit
> Each monster belches from it,
>   We'll know that we are dead.

There is force as well as eloquence in these lines; they prove that Betjeman, contrary to Lord Birkenhead's view, is not altogether 'lacking in the cruelty and spite that are inseparable from [the satirist's] art'. Indignation, even cruelty, is present in another poem, 'Mortality', in which Betjeman gleefully contemplates the death of a senior civil servant in a road accident:

> The first-class brains of a senior civil servant
>   Shiver and shatter and fall
> As the steering column of his comfortable Humber
>   Batters in the bony wall.

It concludes with a line which Tom Driberg felt showed a rather confused understanding of biology:

> The first-class brains of a senior civil servant
>   Are sweetbread on the road today.

The civil servant was, according to Driberg again, a senior Treasury official from whose pedantry and lack of imagination ('I would like to submit for the Minister's concurrence /The following alternative course, /Subject to revision and reconsideration . . .') Betjeman had suffered during his days on the Royal Fine Arts Commission. The lack of pity, however, as well as the verbal infelicities (would a brain shatter?) and the comical inappropriateness of the final line, make this one of Betjeman's least successful poems.

A gentler spirit is detectable in a fine poem from *A Nip in the Air*, 'The Newest Bath Guide' which takes as its epigraph some lines from Christopher Anstey's eighteenth-century poem on the city. Betjeman sonorously regrets the despoliation of old Bath, the insensitive rebuilding of recent years, the penny-pinching schemes of planners and bureaucrats which have reduced its 'varied and human' aspect to a 'uniform nothingness'. But here the final lines seem resigned rather than angry.

> Goodbye to old Bath! We who loved you are sorry
> They're carting you off by developer's lorry.

This restraint is more effective than the intemperate savagery of 'Inexpensive Progress' or the pitilessness of 'Mortality'.

In 'Executive', from the same collection, Betjeman brilliantly portrays a typical mid-seventies type and shows that his social antennae are as acute as ever.

> I am a young executive. No cuffs than mine are cleaner;
> I have a Slimline brief-case and I use the firm's Cortina.
> In every roadside hostelry from here to Burgess Hill
> The *maîtres d'hôtel* all know me well and let me sign the
>   bill.
>
> You ask me what it is I do. Well actually, you know,
> I'm partly a liaison man and partly P.R.O.
> Essentially I integrate the current export drive
> And basically I'm viable from ten o'clock till five.

The tone of voice – 'basically I'm viable', 'Essentially I integrate the current export-drive' – and the choice of significant detail – the 'Slimline brief-case', 'the firm's Cortina' – are exactly right, though the poem falls off towards the end as the crisp observation slackens and the young executive degenerates into one of those stock

Betjeman figures, the spiv-cum-speculator, familiar from earlier
poems. While it seems possible that such a sharp young man may
do 'some mild developing' on the side, his manner of announcing
the fact is unconvincing: 'The modern style, sir, with respect, has
really come to stay.' These pompous words would have come better
from the Town Clerk in 'The Town Clerk's Views'; they are
certainly not part of the argot of a young executive.

'County', however, is far from disappointing and shows Betjeman
unexpectedly and devastatingly turning on the landed gentry, a class
previously immune from his withering scorn. The Porkers are rich
vulgarians – 'All pedigree and purse' – insensitive and obtuse; less
innocent and charming than the Pooters whose name theirs resembles.

> Loud talk of meets and marriages
>   And tax-evasion's heard
> In many first-class carriages
>   While servants travel third.
> 'My dear, I have to spoil them too –
>   Or who would do the chores?
> Well, here we are at Waterloo,
>   I'll drop you at the Stores.'
>
> God save me from the Porkers,
>   The pathos of their lives,
> The strange example that they set
>   To new-rich farmers' wives
> Glad to accept their bounty
>   And worship from afar,
> And think of them as county –
>   County is what they are.

'County' is something genuinely new in Betjeman's work. It shows
him accepting that the class whose houses he has loved are as
culpable as the sub-rout of speculators, bureaucrats, get-rich-quick
farmers and planners he has previously regarded as the enemy. Such
an apparent volte-face is particularly remarkable in a writer nearing
the end of his life. The picture of the hideous Mr Porker and of his
womenfolk in their pearls and twinsets, gaily dropping the names
of earls, is a recognition that the enemy is now within as well as
without. Materialism – Porker will dine with anyone 'So long as he

is rich' – has become so diffused throughout society that there are
really no oases of civilized values left. It is, quite literally, only God
who can save Betjeman now.

As well as the rather disappointing landscape poems with which
High and Low opened, there are, sadly, other dull and lifeless poems
in these two collections. 'Shattered Image' tells in the blankest of
blank verse the story of a successful public relations officer whose
career is ruined by a sexual offence against a minor. The inordinate
length of the piece and the flatness of the diction, while capable of
being interpreted as legitimate dramatic devices in the context –
confessions, after all, are often boring – succeed only in anaesthe-
tizing sympathy. As the narrative unrolls, an inevitable boredom
sets in. On the other hand, there are poems which seem too
narrowly personal to have much impact. 'Anglo-Catholic Congresses', from *High and Low*, with its oppressive weight of impenetrable ecclesiastical allusion – 'Kensit threatens and has Sam Gurney
poped?' – recalls the mood of hope at the height of the High Church
movement in the nineteen-twenties, when these Congresses were
held, and a wave of spiritual regeneration was being prophesied.
However, it does so far less movingly than 'The Old Liberals',
which also describes the after-glow of a time when hope ran high
and a better world was in the process of being made.

'Perp. Revival i' the North' is even more impenetrable. Who is
Temple Moore? Why is the poem written in dialect? What is the
significance of the reference to Lord Faversham? A glance at the
'Illustrated Notes on Victorian Architecture' in *First and Last Loves*
tells one that Temple Moore was an architect who designed the
church referred to – though not named – in the poem, St Wilfred's,
Harrogate, and that his pure, chaste neo-perpendicular interiors
recall, for Betjeman, a particular phase in the Church of England
which is associated with Percy Dearmer, the Sarum Rite and the
English Hymnal. The *Peerage* tells one that Lord Faversham had a
house at Nawton in Yorkshire, and one presumes that Temple
Moore designed the chapel there. Even after the references have
been traced, the poem remains a piece of wilful eccentricity.
Nevertheless, there is an impressive vigour as well as humour in the
verse, which is enhanced by the Scottish dialect in which it is written.

> It's a far cry frae Harrogate
> And mony a heathery mile

Tae a stane kirk wi' a wee spire
  An a verra wee south aisle.
The rhododendrons bloom wi'oot
  On ilka Simmer's day,
And it's there the Airl o'Feversham
  Wad hae his tenants pray;
For there's something in the painted roof
  And the mouldings round the door,
The braw bench and the plain font
  That tells o'Temple Moore.

The same could not be said of 'The Hon. Sec.', an elegy which
lacks the dignity and fine restraint of 'I. M. Walter Ramsden'. The
triteness of sentiment and the jingle-like quality of the diction
suggests Patience Strong or Mary Wilson – a writer whom Betjeman
fatuously confessed to admiring and who features in 'A Mind's
Journey to Diss' – rather than Tom Moore or Tennyson.

The Times would never have the space
  For Ned's discreet achievements;
The public prints are not the place
  For intimate bereavements.

A gentle guest, a willing host,
  Affection deeply planted –
It's strange that those we miss the most
  Are those we take for granted.

This is Betjeman at his worst: sentimental, cliché-ridden, as
metrically inventive as the sort of versifying one expects to find on
a Christmas card. Even the verses he has felt obliged to supply as
Poet Laureate – on the investiture of the Prince of Wales, the
wedding of Princess Anne, the Queen Mother's eightieth birthday
– avoid such depths of banality.

In fact, Betjeman is quite capable of turning out respectable pieces
of official or ceremonial verse. 'Inland Waterway', though a very
minor poem, was written for public declamation at the royal
opening of a canal, and shows the landscape poet's eye to be as
cunning as ever. The lines written 'In Memory of George Whitby,
Architect' for recital at his memorial service in Hawksmoor's St
Mary Woolnoth are dignified and solemn without being embarrassing. The verses for state occasions are perhaps best passed over in

silence; though, in 'A Ballad of the Investiture', Betjeman manages to avoid the inevitable pitfall of sounding too much like a bardic descendant of Richard Dimbleby, a sort of Gold Pen in Waiting, by devoting most of the poem to a description of the countryside. This may well be regarded as cheating, though the difficulty of producing verse of this kind which is not actually ludicrous cannot be underestimated. Betjeman has fared no worse than any other modern laureate in his attempts, and his courage in allowing such poems to be printed, in view of the likely critical reaction, is to be admired. They are sincere and honest attempts to discharge an impossible duty.

The best poems in these two collections are about the two subjects which have stimulated much of Betjeman's best writing in the past: love and death. Indeed, a few of these late poems are among the best he has written, fit to stand beside some of the finest poems in *A Few Late Chrysanthemums*. Among the love poems, 'Agricultural Caress' recalls 'The Licorice Fields at Pontefract'. The object of his desire is the gorgeous Pearl, whose body shimmers, lithe and supple as a tiger's, beneath 'uncouth mechanic slacks'. Betjeman's admiration for her athletic physique, however, is mingled, characteristically, with fear and trembling:

> Such arms to take a man and press
> In agricultural caress
> His head to hers, and hold him there
> Deep buried in her chestnut hair.

This Rossetti-like rural goddess and the promise of her vice-like 'caress' proves too much for him and he cries out, as he did in 'Senex', for release, though with little hope that his prayer will be answered:

> God shrive me from this morning lust
> For supple farm girls: if you must,
> Send the cold daughter of an earl –
> But spare me Thelma's sister Pearl!

In other poems from these years, however, Betjeman celebrates the comforts of love achieved. In 'A Russell Flint' (though the girl in question is an English rose rather than one of Flint's typical dark-eyed, brown-skinned odalisques, and her natural habitat is a Sussex teashop rather than the ruin of some Roman bath), a Joan Hunter

Dunn or Myfanwy is seen not through the eyes of an awestruck inferior, fascinated and frightened by fierce feminine charms he does not properly understand, but as a real woman in a real place, promising peace and fulfilment ('Calm rock pool, on the shore of my security'). Although, as in the earlier poems, Betjeman feels the need to establish her as belonging to a particular social class, to fix her in his mind in particular settings and in certain types of clothes, she is a world away from the elemental woman of his fantasies. Nevertheless, a suggestion of masochism remains in his picturing of her as an Angela Brazil prefect, 'thrillingly kind and stern'.

> I could see you in a Sussex teashop,
>   Dressed in peasant weave and brogues,
> Turning over, as firelight shone on brassware,
>   Last year's tea-stained *Vogues*.
>
> I could see you as a large-eyed student,
>   Frowning as you tried to learn,
> Or, head flung back, the confident girl prefect,
>   Thrillingly kind and stern.

The exquisitely lyrical, 'Lenten Thoughts of a High Anglican' is the best of these late love poems. It is, a footnote explains, about a woman Betjeman has seen in a London church which he sometimes attends. Though he concludes that she must be somebody's mistress – 'Because she has more of a cared-for air /Than many a legal wife' – he sees no profanity in the appearance of such a woman in church. On the contrary, her physical perfection – though, typically, her upper-class voice and expensive clothes are part of her attraction for him – seems almost to aid worship:

> How elegantly she swings along
>   In the vapoury incense veil;
> The angel choir must pause in song
>   When she kneels at the altar rail.

Though the priest might think it 'unorthodox and odd', Betjeman confesses that he sees in the Mistress 'A hint of the Unknown God'. The Neoplatonists believed that the body reflected the soul's perfection and Betjeman has mischievously recorded that he finds his own views supported by so sound a Protestant theologian as Tillich, in a note to the poem written for the sleeve of his record, with music by Mr Jim Parker, *Betjeman's Banana Blush*. Similarly, the wry irony of the title is delectable: his admiring glances at such an expensively kept woman are hardly suggestive of abstinence or self-denial, the tenets of the season.

Another love poem, 'The Cockney Amorist', beautifully conveys a mood of haunting sadness. It is as poignant as that delightful cameo from *New Bats in Old Belfries*, 'In a Bath Teashop'. Tender and understated, it describes the forgotten pleasures of vintage London which seem sad and meaningless now that the lover finds himself alone:

> No more the Hackney Empire
> Shall find us in its stalls
> When on the limelit crooner
> The thankful curtain falls,
> And soft electric lamplight
> Reveals the gilded walls.
>
> I will not go to Finsbury Park
> The putting course to see
> Nor cross the crowded High Road
> To Williamsons' to tea,
> For these and all the other things
> Were part of you and me.

The heartrending sadness of the final stanza, despite the almost comical plainness of the language, faithfully delivers the authentic shock of genuine emotion:

> I love you, oh my darling,
> And what I can't make out
> Is why since you have left me
> I'm somehow still about.

'Good-bye' and 'Five o'Clock Shadow', from *High and Low*, return to the subject of Betjeman's obsessive worrying about death. Neither poem, however, comes near 'Before the Anaesthetic' or even 'The Cottage Hospital'. The element of self-pity, which almost ruins the latter poem, boils over here. Lord Birkenhead hit the nail on the head when he described both poems as 'a wallow in the atmosphere of the Men's Ward'. Betjeman, like Webster, is much obsessed by death; though the very stridency of his night fears sometimes militates against his art. In these two poems, the agony is laid on with a trowel so that one passes over them, unimpressed and unmoved.

Far more successful are the poems in *A Nip in the Air* which show Betjeman calmer and more reconciled as he faces the inevitable fact of death. In 'Loneliness', the air is suddenly crowded with the sound of church bells ringing out:

> You fill my heart with joy and grief –
> Belief! Belief! And unbelief . . .
> And, though you tell me I shall die,
> You say not how or when or why.

Although the bells, as they have done in so many of his poems, suggest 'Our loneliness, so long and vast', Betjeman seems to derive some comfort in this poem from the natural world, the constant cycle of renewal which is suggested in the images of spring, flowering and growth. They help to allay his fears, reminding him that he, too, is part of this natural cycle. Such thoughts do not entirely soften the harsh inevitability of his fate, though a spirit of reconciliation is discernible, an acceptance of the cycle, of birth and death. There is a laconic humour, a wry nod in the direction of infinity, reminiscent in its spare, salty wisdom of Robert Frost, in the lines 'For, sure as blackthorn bursts to snow, /Cancer in some of us will grow'.

In 'Fruit', one of his most beautiful lyrics, images of natural beauty induce a mood reminiscent of Arnold's 'The bloom is gone, and with the bloom go I'. Once again, there is a sense of contentment and resignation, a patient willingness to wait. Much as he loves this world, he seems no longer to wish to maintain the vain struggle against the dying of the light. There is an impressive calm about the poem, unexpected and welcome in a poet who can so often be accused of self-pity:

> Now with the threat growing still greater within me,
>   The church dead which was hopelessly over-restored,
> The fruit picked from these yellowing Worcestershire orchards
>   What is left to me, Lord?

> To wait until next year's bloom at the end of the garden
>   Foams to the Malvern Hills, like an inland sea,
> And to know that its fruit, dropping in autumn stillness,
>   May have outlived me.

Although the serenity of these lines can be admired as much as their lyric grace, their sadness is obvious. *A Nip in the Air* appeared when Betjeman was approaching seventy and there is an almost valedictory air about some of these verses. The suggestion of autumnal melancholy contained in the title pervades the whole collection. There are poems such as 'Lenten Thoughts of a High Anglican' which express the joys of living, but the dominant note is one of bitter-sweet sadness, nostalgia and regret. That this should be so is hardly surprising in a poet in whom such feelings have never been far below the surface.

While intimations of mortality have afflicted Betjeman all his life, laughter, as with many sad men, has always been his solace; perhaps because it temporarily precludes his almost obsessive awareness of the essential misery of the human condition. The final poem in the collection – the sort of poem which, following Tennyson's example with 'Crossing the Bar', Betjeman might well insist on being printed last in future collections of his work – reads almost like an epitaph. One hopes it will not be needed for many years.

> I made hay while the sun shone.
>   My work sold.
> Now, if the harvest is over
>   And the world cold,
> Give me the bonus of laughter
>   As I lose hold.

CHAPTER SEVEN

OPENING PEOPLE'S EYES

Betjeman regards his prose writing – much of which has been for newspapers and magazines as well as for television – as no more than a 'means of earning money in order to buy the free time in which to write poetry'. With characteristic self-deprecation, as well as a sort of perverse pride, he used to describe himself in *Who's Who* as a 'poet and hack'. But for all its apparent ephemerality, none of his prose is mere hackwork and, in total, it forms a creditable body of work. Certainly, none of his prose books – with the exception, perhaps, of the *Collins Guide to English Parish Churches* – is very substantial; but all of them are characterized by a freshness and originality of approach, a gracefulness of style and an undertow of playful irony – qualities shown, for instance, in his description of Bournemouth: 'The sea to Bournemouth is incidental, like the bathroom leading out of a grand hotel suite: something which is there because it ought to be, and used for hygienic reasons.'

Although during the course of his writing life he has written on many subjects – he was, for instance, a brilliant novel-reviewer for the *Daily Telegraph* – his best and most durable prose writing has been on architecture; a subject which, as Philip Larkin has said, lies at the core of Betjeman: 'at Betjeman's heart lies not poetry but architecture – or, if the concepts are allowed, a poetry that embraces architecture and an architecture that embraces poetry'. So many of his poems are about places and buildings that the prose writings may be approached almost as a kind of gloss on the poems, explaining many of the apparently obscure architectural references in which they abound: 'Schools by E. R. Robson in the style of Norman Shaw' or 'Hardman and son of Brum had depicted Him in the chancel'. There are, in addition, odd phrases which echo the poems – 'the vast and lake-like reaches of Chichester Harbour' in the essay on 'Hayling Island' from *First and Last Loves* recalls the 'huge and lake-like reaches' of Beaulieu River in 'Youth and Age' from *New Bats in Old Belfries* – as well as fleeting glimpses of what may have been the origins of particular poems: was, for instance, the Miss Jackson who gave musical parties on Boar's Hill, referred to in *An Oxford University Chest*, the source of that fine poem, 'The Old Liberals'? Both poems and prose spring from the same set of interests and preoccupations, exhibit similar strengths and similar weaknesses. Edward Thomas said that his poem 'October' was no more than a translation into verse of one of his lyrical prose descriptions of the English countryside. Had he wished, Betjeman could have done the same with some of his own prose pieces. This is accounted for not by any self-conscious poeticism of diction but rather by similarity of subject and mood.

Betjeman's interest in architecture is not primarily aesthetic or antiquarian. It is the human associations of buildings and places that fascinate him, just as the architectural and topographical associations of people do. He has said that when he meets someone for the first time he wants to know where he came from, the sort of landscape and buildings among which he grew up. This, for Betjeman, is essential data, enabling him to focus on the person, to define and place him. There is nothing clinical about this process: Betjeman is insatiably curious about people. He relishes human diversity as an artist for whom people and their surroundings are the raw material of his art. He is particularly sensitive not only to the human resonances of particular places but to the marks of class revealed in an accent, the choice of a certain word, the exact social or period overtone conveyed by a branded name. For Betjeman, people are not mere bundles of sensations; they are inhabitants of particular places, wearers of certain kinds of clothes, worshippers at particular churches, members of a particular and definable social class. In their capacity for joy and sorrow, they are, of course, incalculable, but they are comprehensible, in part at least, in terms of their external trappings: Drene and Innoxa, a packet of Weights and a

Hillman Minx. The specificity of his references to places and things – a town is never just a town but Leamington or Exeter, just as trees are always forsythia or laburnum and toothpaste is Euthymol – reveals the passionate observer. He uses his proper nouns not in the crassly materialist way of, say, Ian Fleming and his imitators but because they symbolize something more than themselves. Forsythia is indicative not only of suburban gardens, in particular, but may be taken as an emblem of suburbia in general, its security as well as its small-mindedness. Euthymol is evocative of a whole period as well as of a particular social class. Betjeman deploys these symbols throughout his writings with the same skill, and perhaps for a similar purpose, with which T. S. Eliot patched in the literary allusions which form the fabric of *The Waste Land*: 'These fragments I have shored against my ruins'.

It is often argued that Betjeman's interest in the way people talk and dress is merely snobbish, that the people and places which interest him are either middle class (when a certain air of conde-scension is apparent) or upper class. Certainly, these are the classes which Betjeman knows best. Betjeman's Britain, however, consists of populous seaside resorts as well as prosperous spas and laurel-girt suburbs; industrial cities as well as market towns. His topographical curiosity is all-embracing and is not confined to what is merely beautiful, still less to what is historically important. Propelled by his passionate interest in anything which is expressive of human beings, he has uncovered neglected beauties in non-conformist chapels and in railway stations as well as in such unpromising locations as Leeds, Aberdeen and the Isle of Man. Because of their rich human content, he loves towns and cities as much if not more than the unpeopled Cornish coast and the 'consolingly disastrous' Atlantic which pounds it.

The extent to which Betjeman is moved by the literary associations of a particular place or by straightforward nostalgia for a vanished age should not be forgotten. He is an extremely bookish man: a reader of poetry and of folios of architectural and topographical views, both of which have nourished his love of buildings. He is a lover of the past though no history snob. In that beautiful essay, 'Winter at Home', from *First and Last Loves*, he says: 'There is too much I want to read, too many memories I wish to experience'. It is the past, the pleasures of recollection which stir his imagination. The present is merely the space in which to indulge memory, and the future only to be contemplated with equanimity if it is seen as an unexplored storehouse of memories yet to come. Although he is passionately interested in the signs of contemporary life which he encounters when visiting a place, it is the evidences of the past to be found in the back alleys and the nearer suburbs which really move him. His uniqueness lies in the fusion of these two interests: curiosity about the present and love of the past.

Betjeman's interest in architecture as the background to people's lives makes him as original and distinctive a commentator on architecture as he is a poet. In 1937, he wrote: 'architecture means not a house, or a single building, or Sir Herbert Baker, or the glass at Chartres, but your surroundings; not a town or a street, but our whole over-populated island'. Places are full of emotional significance for Betjeman; buildings are not objects – beautiful or ugly, interesting or uninteresting – but a vital part of experience, the background against which life is lived. In his Rede Lecture on *The English Town in the Last Hundred Years*, given at Cambridge in 1956, he puts this point of view more plainly: 'Looking at places is not for me just going to the church or the castle or the places mentioned in the guidebooks, but walking along the streets and lanes as well, just as in a country house I do not like to see the state rooms only, but the passage to the billiard room, where the Spy cartoons are, and the bedrooms where I note the hairbrushes of the owner and the sort of hair-oil he uses'. In short, he is not so much interested in architecture *qua* architecture as in the life which is lived within it; an Adam ceiling is inseparable from the copies of *Country Life*, trays of drinks and walking sticks beneath; just as a railway can only be properly appreciated in terms of the people who use it.

This approach, instinctive with Betjeman, has gained ground among academic writers in recent years. For instance, Mark Girouard's *Life in the English Country House*, as its title suggests, treats houses not as exemplars of particular architectural styles but in terms of the life lived within them. It is hardly surprising that the emphasis should have shifted in this direction, for architecture is pre-eminently a social art. Betjeman, of course, is an amateur. But he is as far removed from the connoisseur-aesthete, such as Sacheverell Sitwell, who seeks out beauty and visual sensation and fastidiously analyses his response to it, as he is from the trained scholar concerned only with dates and attributions and styles, the sort of dry-as-dust antiquarian who has now disappeared but who was very much in evidence at the time when Betjeman began to write. It is his interest in the human associations of buildings rather than their conformity or non-conformity with some arbitrary rule of taste that has led him to find beauty of a sort in buildings which at one time (until Betjeman started writing, perhaps) were not even considered to be architecture at all – Victorian railway stations and non-conformist chapels. In fact, his enthusiasm for such buildings has succeeded in creating what might be described almost as a revolution in taste, a new way of seeing. His writings and broadcasts have opened people's eyes to the neglected beauties of the encaustic tiles which decorate Gothic Revival churches, the patterned brick of nineteenth-century railway sheds, the engraved mirrors in station waiting-rooms, the moulding on cast-iron lamp standards, the lettering on tin advertisements. He has a most acute eye for detail of this sort. But, though he sees beauty in these well-crafted artefacts, his pleasure in them is not purely aesthetic. They are soaked in human associations, either because they remind him of his own childhood or because they move him to reflect on the transitoriness of human life, such things being poignant reminders of bygone lives. Because the artefacts have proved more durable than the lives they were part of, they have, for Betjeman, the innate sadness of survivals. Once again, it is what they represent rather than what they are which resonates.

It is hardly surprising that one who sees buildings and places primarily in terms of the people who inhabit them should have been drawn to the suburbs, an environment which, as J. M. Richards in his brilliant anatomy of suburbia, *The Castles on the Ground*, observed, 'can only be sympathetically viewed in relation to the lives and interests of [the people who live there]. The suburban style is not a style of architecture but the setting of suburban life itself, and its "taste" is but the local colour the inhabitants gather round themselves in accordance with their peculiar instincts and aspirations.' Suburbia can be viewed sympathetically *only* as a projection of the tastes of its inhabitants, and Betjeman has sought out the same human, relative and atmospheric attributes in other places – take, for instance, his essay on 'Cheltenham' – which offend less against the accepted canons of taste. The discovery and sympathetic presentation of suburbia with its speckled laurels, tile-hung gables, dormers glimpsed behind monkey puzzles, green-houses and conservatories is an inevitable function of his interest in the human associations of places but it is by no means his only achievement.

In fact, Betjeman's most important contribution as a writer on architecture has been his almost single-handeḍ rehabilitation of the Victorians. In a preface to the 1949 edition of his pioneer study of *The Gothic Revival*, Kenneth Clark pays handsome tribute to Betjeman – 'one of the few original minds of our generation' – for 'his sensitive response to architecture, as to everything which expresses human needs and affections [and] which allowed him to see through the distorting fog of fashion'. He goes on to say that the revised view of Victorian architecture 'is due directly to the stimulus of his talk . . . the radiation of a single personality'. Betjeman was certainly one of the first to recognize the merits of Victorian architecture, which had previously been dismissed as monstrous, ugly, vulgar and grotesquely sentimental like the age which gave it birth. The prejudice took a long time to die. Even Clark was rather worried that Betjeman's 'adventurous spirit' might lead to the glorification of buildings remarkable for nothing but the fact that they were erected in the nineteenth century. Betjeman's taste in Victorian building is certainly catholic. Though by no means undiscriminating, he finds more to love than to hate. He does not reserve his admiration for the less characteristic examples of Victorian design such as Paxton's Crystal Palace – 'the first prefab', and admired as such by twentieth-century functionalists – or austere masterpieces such as Cubitt's King's Cross Station which is, essentially, a modern building in its absence of extraneous ornament, its puritanical rejection of historicism and its sense of 'fitness for purpose'. He relishes, uninhibitedly, the full-blooded masterpieces of Victorian architecture which have only recently been allowed into the pantheon; partly as a result of Betjeman's advocacy and partly as a result of dissatisfaction with the soulless anonymity of so much twentieth-century architecture. He admires the richness, elaboration, adamantine self-confidence, sound craftsmanship and fertile invention of Victorianism at its most flamboyant: Scott's St Pancras Hotel whose gigantic presence and arrogantly beautiful skyline does not admit of a lukewarm response; Butterfield's Keble College with its violent, if invigorating, colour scheme; Crossland's splendidly plutocratic Royal Holloway College – 'in Portland stone and red brick, vaster and more elaborate than Chambord and set among pines and rhododendrons of Surrey'; the bold, vertiginous massing of Colcutt's now mutilated Imperial Institute which, in defiance of the purists, he upheld as a 'new version of the Renaissance style'.

Betjeman believes that Victorian architecture must be approached by way of its architects; for it is expressive of their personalities in a way that the architecture of no other period is. These remarkable men held strong views about the buildings which they designed. For them architecture partook of religion and morality, both powerful forces in nineteenth-century England, with the result that Scott's disagreements with Palmerston over the style in which the new government offices in Whitehall were to be built were as intense as Michelangelo's battles with the Pope. In architects such as George Edmund Street, Gilbert Scott, and William Butterfield, the spirit of the age in all its richness and diversity, an age of great creative achievement and unbelievable industry, is at work. These men flourished before the dawn of specialism and the advent of the expert; before the age of economic constraint and the conveyor belt. They were great individualists and Betjeman admires them not only for their achievements but as rich personalities in themselves: Street, affable, unpretentious and sincere; Scott, incredibly busy, telegraphing his London office from the provinces to ask 'Why am I here?'; Butterfield, austere and celibate, ruthlessly correcting his draughtsmen's drawings in ink, mounting the scaffolding on site only after it had been dusted by his workmen; Norman Shaw, wearing extra-long shirt cuffs so that he could sketch out a design if he found himself sitting next to a prospective client at dinner. They belonged to the era before the compulsory registration of architects, when architecture was still an art and a craft rather than a profession. Betjeman prefers them to the constructional engineers who have emerged in their place. One of the many reasons why he admired Sir Ninian Comper, the church architect, was that he continued to describe himself as 'architect, not registered' in *Who's Who* until his death in 1960. The expert, the professional, has always seemed a desiccated and unappetizing breed to Betjeman.

In all his writings on Victorian architecture, it is the vitality of the detail as much as the magnificence of the whole which commands his attention: the crispness of carvings, the skilful moulding of terracotta ornament, the sensitive use of local materials, the daring use of colour in Minton tiles and polychromatic brick. This decorative richness and tradition of craftsmanship has been lost in the twentieth century with the rise of an international style and the techniques of mass production. Although Betjeman does not condemn all modern buildings, he knows that the cheapness and dullness of the materials available to modern architects counts against them. He points out that many of the illustrations of twentieth-century buildings in his *Pictorial History of English Architecture* (1972) are put in 'as cautionary examples – not because I admire them all'. In the public mind, at least, Betjeman is seen as the arch-opponent of modernism, and the most indefatigable preservationist. During the thirties, he opposed the demolition of eighteenth- and nineteenth-century buildings in London to make way for department stores and office blocks, and in the sixties he led the campaign to preserve Hardwick's Euston Propylaeum, earning his supporters the title 'Betjemanic depressives'. Some people regard his campaigns as merely sentimental and nostalgic but now we all know – or should know – that any old building which is pulled down, however unexceptional it is by the standards of its own age, is almost certain to be replaced by something worse. The new Euston is hideous — 'a disastrous and inhuman structure', in Betjeman's words – and probably a less efficient building than the old one. By the same token, the high-rise flats which disfigure every city in the country, though once endorsed by progressive architects as the ideal machines for living, are, we now recognize, neither so nice to look at nor to live in as the little streets of terraced houses which they replaced. John Press has suggested that Betjeman would agree with Hardy's remark that rebuilding and reconstruction destroy the 'sentiment of association' and lead inevitably to 'a rupture of continuity' so that people feel displaced, robbed of their familiar surroundings and made strangers in a strange land. It is his sense that our surroundings are important to us rather than mere antiquarianism which has made Betjeman so keen to preserve buildings which planners, in pursuit of some abstract and inhuman ideal, have sought to destroy. Betjeman, in fact, has never had any time for what he once called 'antiquarian prejudice' and despises the person who seeks to preserve something for no other reason than that it is old. What he objects to is the destruction of the human scale and distinctive local atmosphere of a place in the name of some such bureaucratic fiction as 'urban renewal'; the wilful destruction of something which is pleasing to make way for something which is not.

The most common criticism of Betjeman the architectural critic and preservationist is that he is a romantic with no conception of the problems of modern architects and no interest in, say, the housing of the working classes. Certainly, he has had some eccentric ideas on the subject. In the thirties, he suggested that Nuffield's pressed steel factory in Oxford should make 'portable houses' which could be moved 'from one place to another when they were wanted'. They sound like caravans without wheels. Such a prescription suggests that Betjeman, quite literally, wanted this particular problem simply to go away. He was also fond of striking out against the cheaper kind of suburban house which he seemed to think was built exclusively of unseasoned timber and doomed to fall down within a few years. In fact, these jerry-built, inter-war suburbs have matured into extremely pleasant places in which to live, as Betjeman would now admit. His hatred of this kind of building may, in part, be explained by his partial conversion to more progressive architectural ideas during his time on the *Architectural Review*.

He expounded some of these ideas in his lecture, 'Antiquarian Prejudice', given at the Group Theatre in 1937 and subsequently issued as one of the Hogarth Press's Sixpenny Pamphlets. In it, he came out strongly in favour of purity of design and castigated the 'antiquarian prejudice' which refused to see merit in any building erected since the sixteenth century. He linked this attitude of mind with 'jazz modernism' which he saw as the illegitimate offspring of antiquarianism. 'Antiquarian prejudice' derived from a failure of taste just as 'jazz modernism' derived from a failure of nerve. Establishment architects, who used columns and porticoes as surface decoration to add dignity to their banks, town halls and head offices, were guilty of misunderstanding tradition; the spec builders and purveyors of art deco were debasing modern architecture with their cheap and nasty decorative schemes, all lower case lettering and chromium plating, because of a similar misunderstanding. The 'jazz modernism' which annoyed Betjeman so is still to be seen, looking rather pock-marked and dishevelled, in those all-white, 'cubistic', corner-window-style filling stations and private houses – by Bauhaus out of spec builder – which survive by many roadsides.

Betjeman's 'advanced' ideas on architecture were very much to the fore in his first prose book, *Ghastly Good Taste* (1933) which J. M. Richards, Betjeman's successor on the *Architectural Review* and one of the best apologists for modern architecture, described as 'an entertaining and sometimes savage analysis of contemporary taste'. It is a very short book and shows some signs of having been hastily written. It was intended as something of a manifesto and this gives it a rather dated air: credos seldom keep. Betjeman now feels that he was showing off in the book, pretending to be up to date whilst secretly preferring the architecture of almost any other age to that of his own. Certainly, apart from a few incidental delights such as the parodic extracts from Batty Langley's correspondence with Lord Ongley (Frederick Etchells played Langley to Betjeman's Ongley) and the fine opening chapter describing the plight of the twentieth-century owner of a great house, it is the book's pretty appearance and the folding illustration by Peter Fleetwood-Hesketh depicting architecture's 'progress' from Christendom to Big Business and Chaos which stay in the mind rather than the text. There are a few factual errors, uncharacteristic of the later Betjeman, and some disconcerting eccentricities of judgement – praising William Morris but not Philip Webb, for instance – which were picked up by H. S. Goodhart-Rendel, himself a rather idiosyncratic commentator on Victorian architecture, in a review of the new edition issued in 1970. Betjeman took the opportunity to revise many of the opinions expressed in the original edition for this reprint. His extremely hostile view of Norman Shaw ('The less said of this gentleman the better. He was a facile, expensive and pretentious architect, who, like many of his followers, had a facility for catching rich clients.') was turned on its head. His rash approval of several contemporary buildings was withdrawn. He had said that, because Gibbs had the boldness to erect the classical Radcliffe Camera in the middle of a gothic city during the eighteenth century, he would today, 'have had the courage to build as sincere an essay in modern materials in its place'. In 1970, he pointed out that he had come to regard this opinion as fallacious, 'the only excuse Colonel Seifert can make for Centre Point'. Perhaps the only opinions in the book with which Betjeman now feels comfortable are those about the need for the ordinary man not to be intimidated by the expert's insistence that he knows best and his praise for the grace and elegance of Regency architecture (still his favourite style), its great town-planning schemes such as Cheltenham, Brighton, and the Nash terraces in Regent's Park, and its industrial architecture, such as St Katharine's Docks, which Betjeman describes as 'so plain as to be "modern", so useful as to be terrifying'. He condemns the 'prettifying' tendency of architects such as Batty Langley which led eventually to the stylistic mish-mash of lower suburbia. Inevitably, too, he derides the 'jazz modernism' of, say, the Hoover Factory – though, paradoxically, such buildings have now acquired the sort of period charm which a latter-day Betjeman might find appealing – but singles out for praise the clean-limbed functional style of buildings by architects such as Wells Coates and Frederick Etchells, the translator of Le Corbusier's *Towards a New Architecture*, which were praised in the enlightened pages of the *Architectural Review*.

Betjeman seems to be calling, in what is frequently a confusing book, for a return to stylistic integrity and the repudiation of contemporary barbarities. Though his message is unexceptionable, he is not the most effective of propagandists. His mind is too quirky; he is too sensitive and humane to be the man to lead a crusade. His praise of those modern buildings which exemplify the new virtues – plainness and honesty – seems, furthermore, a good deal less passionate than his praise of chosen buildings from the past. One senses what he later confirmed, that his loyalties lay elsewhere. The praise accorded to even the finest of modern buildings was put in, perhaps, to appease more progressive friends and colleagues. Even as a young man, Betjeman was never quite in tune with the times in which he lived. As J. M. Richards has said: 'His speciality was everything Victorian.' As his principal interest, at this time, was in the architects of the Arts and Crafts movement – Voysey, Ashbee and Mackintosh – his deep knowledge of this period could be used in the pages of the *Architectural Review* 'to enlighten its readers about the history and origins of the new architecture, especially the roots the latter could be shown to have in the revolution the Arts and Crafts architects had created in rejecting the academic conventions of their own time'. But while the first stirring of the modern movement interested and delighted him, he was always, in his heart of hearts, deeply unsympathetic to the so-called international style which evolved from it.

The grand historical generalizations in which the book deals, the flimsy historical schema – Gothic architecture, pure and confident, flourishing in an age of faith, followed by the Renaissance and the dawn of self-consciousness, leading inevitably to pluralistic imitativeness and stylistic confusion – also seem rather makeshift and unconvincing. His final plea for a return to true architectural values, responsive to contemporary needs, in order to displace the shallow

eclecticism favoured by so many of the more successful architects
of the older generation similarly fails to carry much conviction.
Betjeman's mind turns naturally to the small, the particular, the
local rather than the grand, the general, the universal. When we are
told that 'architecture can only be made alive again by a new order
and another Christendom', we feel that we are being addressed by
a pinchbeck Ruskin and not by Betjeman. Such a view suggests a
kind of totalitarianism, superficially attractive in a socially frag-
mented and culturally insecure age, but carrying dangers of its own
as can be seen in the results of the doctrinaire experiments of
modern architects which now disfigure all our towns and cities.
Ghastly Good Taste, though on the whole an interesting and
entertaining polemic, does not represent Betjeman at his best or
most typical. It did, however, serve its purpose of establishing his
name as a writer on architecture.

The characteristic virtue of his best writings on architecture is his
ability to respond to a place or a building in terms of its human
associations. His little books, *Vintage London* (1942) and *English
Cities and Small Towns* (1943) are nostalgic evocations of places he
has known and loved and which he now sees as endangered by
greed and speculation. In his view, London and the other English
cities and towns stood in as much danger from bureaucratic high-
handedness, the desire to destroy the picturesque accumulation of
centuries and to replace it with a standardized dream of municipal
tidiness as they did from German bombs. He criticizes the 'easy
generalization about the new world after this war, [the] silly
assumption that everything old must be pulled down and we must
all live in skyscrapers made of glass and steel'. He could not believe
that the nation was fighting to usher in such 'textureless materialism'. There can be no doubt, however, that Betjeman must now
regard his campaign as lost in all save a few places. Though
he shows as much relish for battle as ever, he now knows that he
can only hope for tactical victories. In strategic terms, he has
been defeated, as we all have, by the ineluctable logic of progress.

His collection of essays, topographical and architectural, *First and
Last Loves* (1952) was prefaced by a diatribe against the common
man called 'Love is Dead' which, in John Summerson's opinion,
constituted 'one of the most savage jeremiads on English life today
which I have ever read'. In this essay, Betjeman detects the hand of

the common man, or rather 'the average man, which is far worse', everywhere. His natural home is suburbia, a hideous makeshift suburbia of the soul which stifles individuality, creativity, even love, and replaces them with good taste, uniformity, moderation in all things, total indifference: 'He is our ruler and he rules by commit- tees. He gives us what most people want, and he believes that what is popular is best . . . He is the Lowest Common Multiple, not even the Highest Common Factor. And we have put him in charge of us, whatever his political party at the moment'. Because the effects of this levelling, neutralizing tendency have spread everywhere, the essays in *First and Last Loves* celebrate an England which can now only be seen in odd surviving patches. The places which Betjeman loves are those in which the traditional life of the community goes on despite prevailing barbarism, and they are getting fewer. These seaside towns, spas, and market towns are oases in a desert of concrete and Betjeman pays homage to them as he describes their characteristic beauties. The book is both a celebration and a lament, as all his books are.

The essay on 'London Railway Stations' from this collection is one of Betjeman's finest achievements in prose. These buildings, as well as being beautiful in themselves, are full of memories for Betjeman. Each has a distinct personality of its own which is created not so much by the architecture as by the people who use it: Waterloo with its servicemen, race-goers and top civil servants; Victoria with 'the flashiest of all suburban travellers' from Brighton; Liverpool Street with its workmen's trains bound for Tottenham, Wanstead and Edmonton; Charing Cross, whose travellers like to give the impression 'that they are going abroad'; Cannon Street, 'my favourite, so echoing, so lofty and so sad'; Broad Street, full of 'ghosts of frock-coated citizens who once crowded the old North London trains'; King's Cross, full of expense-account civil servants returning to Scotland; St Pancras, 'a station apart . . . still the aristocrat route to Scotland'; Euston, for the Irish; Marylebone, quiet and unused; Paddington, full of Oxford dons, schoolboys and country people. It is Betjeman's ability to apprehend the meaning of a building or a place which is his real achievement as a prose writer. As Osbert Lancaster wrote: 'Any industrious fool with a good reference library can docket and classify a work of art, but to transmit it as an experience shared is an infinitely rare gift'. Betjeman, though he pays tribute to sensitive scholars such as Sir

John Summerson, has no time for fact-grubbing mediocrities
afflicted by what he has described in a happy phrase as 'foot and
note disease'. Yet the range and depth of his knowledge are
considerable, as is evident even in the occasional pieces on architecture which he wrote for the *Daily Telegraph* during the early sixties.

As with his poetry, it is England – with occasional excursions
into other parts of the British Isles – which provides the canvas for
Betjeman's prose writing. He has said that he feels 'frustrated by
ignorance' when he surveys foreign buildings. He does not mean
that he knows nothing about foreign architecture but that he does
not know enough about the whole community – 'its history, its
class distinctions, and its literature' – to be able to make a proper
response to its buildings. Architecture is, after all, a social and not
an abstract art. Betjeman's lack of interest in foreign locations is not
a case of insularity or narrow parochialism despite Evelyn Waugh's
dismissal of his celebration of the obscure, the neglected, the local
as both sentimental and naïve.

In a review of *First and Last Loves*, Waugh accused Betjeman, who
had attacked suburban mediocrity in 'Love is Dead', of himself
'leading the fashionable flight from greatness, away from the
traditional hierarchy of classic genius, away from the library to the
third box of the second-hand bookseller, away from the Mediter-
ranean to the Isle of Man, away from the universal church into odd
sects and schisms, away from historic places into odd corners of
Aberdeen'. Though this reads like a definitive condemnation of
Betjeman's little Englandism as well as of his double standards, there
is less inconsistency in Betjeman · than Waugh supposes. He is
interested in what is expressive of human needs and aspirations.
Aberdeen and the Isle of Man, Lyndhurst and Ventnor, speak more
eloquently of these needs to Betjeman than Paris or Rome. Truth,
for him, is not to be found in a 'traditional hierarchy' but in what
individual human beings do in their daily lives, and he gets the
sense of human life as it actually is lived in such obscure places. It
is the sense of unimportant lives carrying on regardless which
nourishes his art rather than the classic virtues pompously catalogued
by Waugh. Though such places as he describes in his essays have no
place in European civilization as Waugh understands it, they are,
nevertheless, authentically human and, as such, important to
Betjeman. He attacks the 'average man' not because of his remoteness from a supposed classical tradition but because of his denial

of what is human and his elevation of what is efficient, hygienic or just plain 'good for you' in its place.

The essays in *First and Last Loves* are a plea for diversity, for everything that is sanctified by human use against what is merely smart or fashionable or 'in good taste'. They are congeneric with the poems; prose manifestations of the same unique sensibility. The essay on 'Cheltenham' says no more than the poem of the same title, though it does so with the addition of names and dates; a poem such as 'Henley-on-Thames' would fit well enough into the section called 'Coast and Country' just as the poem 'St Saviour's, Aberdeen Park, Highbury, London, N.' is in very much the same style (description followed by affirmation), as the prose pieces on Blisland, Mildenhall and St Mark's, Swindon; 'The Metropolitan Railway' or 'Monody on the Death of Aldersgate Street Station' are almost companion pieces to the essay on 'London Railway Stations'; the essay on 'Nonconformist Architecture' illuminates and complements a poem such as 'Competition'. Betjeman's simple, unadorned prose – short, simple sentences, shorn of ornament but able to comprehend nostalgic evocation, precise description and passionate invective – is a delight in itself, but the sincerity of the response to buildings and landscapes, ordinary enough in themselves, genuinely extends experience.

Before the appearance of these essays, *An Oxford University Chest* (1938), its title derived from the name which Oxford gives to its treasury, had been his most substantial prose work. It was a particularly lavish production, a coffee-table book with some interesting and unusual photographs by the Bauhaus refugee Lazlo Moholy-Nagy, as well as brilliant cartoons by Osbert Lancaster. The first part of the book consists of three linked essays on Oxford with particular reference to the University rather than to 'Christminster' (according to Betjeman, the market town which it had largely displaced) or to 'Motopolis', the creation of 'William Morris the second', as Betjeman calls him, which, in its turn, seemed to be trying to displace the University. There are some rather patronizing comments about the sort of dim undergraduate who fights his way to Oxford from a grammar school and some in-jokes at the expense of hearty dons and the English school in which Betjeman had himself suffered. The tone of this opening section is very much that of the pieces on university life Betjeman might have contributed to *Cherwell*. In short, he likes witty, stylish dons, the richer sort of undergraduate and the sort of scout who looks up to undergraduates who spend more time over their lunch than over their books. It all has a rather gruesomely dated air today. In fact, the best part of the book is the 'Architectural Tour' which lists in double-columned pages the principal sights of the city in alphabetical order. It is no mere catalogue, for the comments are both witty and piquant as well as informative. It could still be used as a guide to the city by a curious visitor.

Betjeman has been a writer of guidebooks all his professional life – the Shell Guides in the thirties and Murray's Architectural Guides in the forties as well as numerous pamphlets, such as his Pitkin Guide to the City churches, since then. Because his most intense aesthetic experiences have come from *looking* at buildings – 'a public art gallery which is always open' – it is natural that he should wish to stimulate and inform people who are keen to visit and see rather than merely to study. The *Collins Guide to English Parish Churches*, his most solid achievement as a writer on architecture, is most definitely a guidebook designed to be carried about in glove-compartment or saddle-bag rather than perused in the study. Although the book is a team effort with many contributors, it bears Betjeman's stamp throughout; his was the baton which orchestrated the many and diverse talents which were brought together in order to make the book. He contributed the long introductory essay, a masterpiece of its kind and described by Sir Arthur Bryant as 'one of the finest pieces of historical reconstruction I have ever read', and wrote most of the essays which preface the sections on individual counties as well as many of the descriptive notes on individual churches, particularly those in Berkshire, Oxfordshire and Corn-wall, the counties which he knows best. With its system of star ratings, reminiscent of the *Good Food Guide* (an asterisk denotes an 'exceptionally attractive church', a very unscholarly and subjective sort of description), there can be no doubt that the *Guide* is intended to promote enjoyment. In Betjeman's opinion, 'church-crawling is the richest of pleasures'. The descriptive notes are less detailed than those in Pevsner's *Buildings of England*, to which Betjeman inevitably pays tribute, and emphasis is placed on the setting of the church and its 'atmosphere'. For instance, the church of St Mark and St Luke at Avington in Cornwall is described with hardly a mention of styles or dates (compare the mock-serious description of 'Tickleby Tomcat' in *Antiquarian Prejudice*): 'Almost alone among the trees at the end of a lane and beside the River Kennet; towerless, aisleless and mostly Norman; dark, mysterious and ancient-looking inside with rich Norman carving'. For Betjeman, the book was a labour of love and might have been inscribed, like the oval boards he saw hanging in Somerton church: TO GOD'S GLORY & THE HONOR OF THE CHURCH OF ENGLAND. The long introduction which contains some of his best prose is his tribute to the faith which has sustained him despite the 'many moments of doubt when the only thing which buoys me up is the thought that I would sooner the Incarnation were true than that it were not' as well as to the buildings whose beauty led him to that faith.

His most recent books – *A Pictorial History of English Architecture* and *London's Historic Railway Stations* – were both published in 1972. Both originated as articles commissioned for magazines and both are beautifully illustrated on the principle that 'one good photograph is worth ten pages of text'. The first is a masterpiece of compression, the second an expansion of his brilliant essay on London's termini from *First and Last Loves*. The visual splendour of the two books serves to remind us that Betjeman has made many television programmes on architectural and topographical subjects; indeed was a pioneer in this field and set a standard upon which his successors have had difficulty in improving. The most celebrated of his television films is *Metro-land*, an undoubted broadcasting classic, which attains heights of lyrical evocation rarely achieved in this medium. The use of verse in the script of such a programme might seem, on the face of it, a self-indulgent and, indeed, potentially embarrassing device. In fact, it succeeds wonderfully. In the passage describing the villas of St John's Wood, a vanished age is magically evoked not by rehearsal of facts but by an exercise in imaginative sympathy:

> And here, screened by shrubs,
> Walled-in from public view,
> Lived the kept women.
> What puritan arms have
>   stretched within these rooms
> To touch what tender breasts,
> As the cab-horse stamped in the
>   road outside.

While it would not be true to say that Betjeman's prose writing is as important as his poetry, it is by no means inconsiderable. He has brought an original sensibility to bear on his subject which has commanded the respect of scholars such as Clark and Summerson as well as the admiration of the general public. He has helped to create a revolution in taste which has had lasting consequences on the way in which we all perceive our surroundings. His real achievement, however, has been to encourage people 'to find excitement by using their eyes, and to stop and look at buildings'. More than any other writer and broadcaster on architecture he has encouraged the diffusion of this particular kind of pleasure. Even if he had never written a line of poetry, we should still have heard of him.

CHAPTER EIGHT

THE LIMITS
OF WHAT'S HUMAN

Intellectuals who admire Betjeman are sometimes rather puzzled by the fact. Certainly, he is accomplished and enjoyable; but he remains, for them at least, something of an enigma: 'unique', 'unclassifiable', 'no one quite like him' are words they use to describe him. In admitting to enjoyment of his verse they are conscious of a certain robust perversity in themselves; they imagine that they are slumming, like the gourmet who says he also likes fish and chips or the Cambridge mathematician who supports West Bromwich Albion. Reading Betjeman, like reading Wodehouse or Fleming, is something one does for fun. Though Betjeman is interesting and unusual, he is irredeemably outside the mainstream of twentieth-century poetry, they say. Just how far outside this supposed mainstream he really is, however, remains a question to be answered.

Mount Zion appeared in the same year as Michael Roberts's *New Signatures*, the anthology which gave a sort of corporate identity to the politically obsessed poets of the thirties. Betjeman was, of course, apolitical; uninterested and unmoved – poetically unmoved, that is – by the great issues of the day: mass unemployment and the rise of Fascism. But, though his poems were personal rather than political; though he was apparently unaware of the impending international crisis (Osbert Lancaster wondered if he had even heard about the Spanish Civil War); unseduced by communism, undisillusioned with liberal democracy; unsympathetic, not to say hostile,

to the idea of direct political action; he nevertheless had close
personal ties with the group of poets led by Auden. What is more,
as Philip Toynbee has observed, the writers of that generation had
no difficulty in accepting Betjeman as a serious artist. In their own
way, his poems were as original and 'modern' as Auden's. Indeed,
there were many resemblances. In matters of form, Auden, Spender,
MacNeice, and Day Lewis were as much traditionalists as Betjeman.
Auden, for instance, was equally fond of adapting hymn metres
and shared Betjeman's enthusiasm for churches and railways, his
curiosity about the ways of the suburban middle classes, and his
interest in public-school lore. And, if Betjeman had a lot in common
with his contemporaries, he was not entirely dissimilar to the poets
who emerged in the fifties. The Movement poets stood for many of
those things which Betjeman's verse could be said to exemplify –
clarity of diction rather than cloudy obscurity, poems about
ordinary life and personal experience rather than poems about other
poets or 'abroad', formal conservatism rather than technical experiment – even though they did not all admire him.

In fact, the view of Betjeman as an oddity, whose charm is
accounted for by his eccentricity, can only be sustained if one accepts
the poetry of Pound and Eliot and their derivatives (comparatively
few, in fact) as the norm of twentieth-century verse and anything
more 'traditional' as a perverse exercise in nostalgia or escapism. It
might be truer to say that Eliot and Pound took poetry into a cultural
ivory tower from which it was partially liberated by Auden and his
associates because their poems had a more direct relation to life as
it was lived and that Betjeman played a part in this process. Eliot's
massive intellect resulted in a sharpening of language as well as of
thought in contemporary poetry, qualities noticeably absent in the
trite, sentimental lyrics of the less inspired Georgian poets. But his
polyglot allusiveness, his spiritual aloofness, was in danger of
becoming a barrier to communication. Indeed, at times, his verse
seemed to be degenerating into a mere intellectual game: Spot the
Allusion. One thinks, for instance, of 'Burbank with a Baedeker:
Bleistein with a Cigar' where echoes, quotations and allusions are
as tight-packed as the supposedly incorrect usages with which
Betjeman stuffed 'How to Get on in Society'. Such a poem was a
dead-end rather than a new beginning.

Similarly, the new Romanticism of the forties with its elevation
of the myth and the image, its respect for the incantatory intensity

of Dylan Thomas, with which Betjeman had nothing in common, soon came to seem old hat as well as pretentious. The corrupt poetic standards of the age were to be seen in the fact that the empty rhetoric of Edith Sitwell's later verse was seriously held up as great poetry. Although it is dangerous to attempt to analyse the course of contemporary poetry as if it were in a constant state of growth and development, there is, in fact, a clear line of descent – from Hardy and Housman through Edward Thomas and the better Georgians, to Auden and on to Larkin – within which Betjeman's *oeuvre* has a certain coherence. He is really only an outsider to the extent that any original poet is. If Betjeman is considered to be out of step with the march of modern poetry, one has first to establish that other poets are in step with each other and second that modern poetry, like a marching army, is, in fact, going somewhere. Both these premises are extremely dubious.

The main reason why Betjeman appears to be outside the mainstream – or, at least, what passes for the mainstream – is that his verse is not amenable to close verbal analysis. Its meaning is clear, there are no complex allusions to be elucidated; apart, that is, from a scattering of architectural and topographical references, though even these poems can be comprehended without such information. In this, he resembles Philip Larkin among contemporary poets: 'I may flatter myself, but in one sense I'm like Evelyn Waugh or John Betjeman in that there's not much to *say* about my work. When you've read a poem, that's it, it's all quite clear what it means.' Among the poets of an older generation, one thinks of Hardy in whose work meaning is similarly accessible. In *Thomas Hardy and British Poetry*, Donald Davie quotes Irving Howe's comment about Hardy (a comment which, *mutatis mutandis*, might be applied to Betjeman): 'Any critic can, and often does, see all that is wrong with Hardy's poetry, but whatever it was that makes for his strange greatness is much harder to describe. Can there ever have been a critic of Hardy who, before poems like "The Going" and "During Wind and Rain", did not feel the grating inadequacy of verbal analysis, and the need to resort to such treacherous terms as "honesty", "sincerity" and even "wisdom"?' Certainly, such treacherous terms occur, as they are bound to do, in my own discussion of Betjeman's poems. The critic of Betjeman can only hope to enhance the reader's enjoyment of the verse; suggest which are the good poems and which are the bad poems; and, thus, attempt to define the nature of Betjeman's achievement. Although one can try to describe what Betjeman has done, he does not need to be interpreted for the general reader in the way that Eliot obviously does. One cannot imagine a *Student's Guide* to Betjeman's *Collected Poems*, without recourse to which the poems may not even be understood let alone enjoyed. The very idea that literature may be regarded as a source of pleasure is, of course, a highly suspect one in some quarters. Few university critics would accept Lord David Cecil's hedonistic assertion that it is the duty of the student of literature to enjoy himself. They would regard such a view as intellectually flabby, hopelessly self-indulgent, a feet-on-the-chimneypiece rather than an elbows-on-the-desk view of literature. Betjeman's lack of appeal for such critics is partially explained by the fact that he affords them no opportunity to show off; no occasion for a dazzling display of erudition or ingenuity with which to impress colleagues and rivals and thereby secure academic prefer-ment. For such critics, the mainstream comprises those writers whom it is possible to teach, or, rather, those whom it is necessary to teach. A text, like a mathematical puzzle, is valued according to the degree of difficulty which it exhibits. This emphasis on difficulty for its own sake has led to the elevation of a number of very dull writers and demotion to the status of middle-brow entertainers of very good writers such as Graham Greene and Evelyn Waugh. The lust for difficulty has, in fact, already resulted in some academics creating 'works of literature' whose only purpose is to be taught in class; these home-grown products are needed because creative writers cannot be trusted to produce work of sufficient complexity nor which lends itself readily to the particular kind of critical exegesis currently in favour. One can imagine that if such a process were to continue, the gap between what students read because they have to and what the general public reads because it chooses to will grow to the extent that a literate layman will be as much at sea when confronted with an Eng. Lit. paper as a normally numerate layman is when confronted with a mathematics paper.

Betjeman is predominantly a giver of pleasure: an entertainer, if you will. The vast sales of *Collected Poems* are accounted for by people who genuinely enjoy reading him or, at the very worst, who have seen him on television and formed the impression that they might. Nobody reads Betjeman because they have to; his poems are read rather than used. But because he is thought of as an entertainer – 'The entertainer par excellence' as Michael Schmidt calls him, without making it clear whether he intends a compliment or a slight – it is assumed that his funny poems are his best. This assumption springs from the mistaken view that what is entertaining must also be comic. In fact, a work of literature may be both entertaining and tragic; a poem by Philip Larkin or a novel by Graham Greene is as unrelentingly gloomy as anything by Beckett, though it is also entertaining which many things by Beckett are not. The pleasure derives from verbal felicity and metrical skill in the one and sheer narrative power in the other; the satisfaction which is felt in the resolution and ordering of experience, and which is central to all art, in both. What is being described is far from pleasant in itself: loss, grief, remorse, failure, guilt, pain; those things most people feel most of the time. Betjeman, like these other writers, is not cosily reassuring for he too confronts these themes in an equally direct manner. But, like them, he is an entertainer in the sense that he manages to communicate with a large audience while offering little for their comfort. Anyone who puts down Betjeman's *Collected Poems* and feels that he has had his smug prejudices confirmed or been given a good laugh has read the wrong poems. Even Lord Birkenhead recognized that Betjeman was 'not a "funny" poet, and resents being regarded as one'.

Those of Betjeman's poems which show him as a light versifier are, for the most part, bad poems by his own standards and not even very good light verse. Yet, although he has disowned such pieces as 'How to Get On in Society', anthologists continue to reprint them. The jolly children's poems such as 'Hunter Trials' are effective enough in their way though they are no more typical of him than *The Little Fire Engine* is of Graham Greene. His satires are often disastrous failures. Betjeman succeeds in being funny only when he is recording his observations – as in 'Beside the Seaside' – never when he is being controversial – as in 'Group Life: Letchworth' or 'Huxley Hall'. A satirist must, as well as having strong intellectual convictions, which Betjeman has not, be something of an outsider: able to regard his fellow humans with a certain detachment; to see them as essentially different from himself or, at least, falling short of some hypothetical standard which he has himself set. Betjeman, on the contrary, relishes human absurdity and regards himself as being as much an exemplar of it as anybody. People interest him;

they do not fill him with disgust as they did Swift. He hates only the cruel and the insensitive and he does not believe that these form the majority of mankind.

He is an accepter rather than a rejecter of life; indeed, his attachment to it is intense. He is capable of writing poems which seem to be pure fun because his enjoyment of life is so keen; just as he is capable of writing hymns to natural beauty because he loves landscape so passionately. It would be wrong to regard him as a solemn writer, as ballads such as 'The Arrest of Oscar Wilde' or breathless love lyrics such as 'Pot Pourri from a Surrey Garden' testify. But what is a source of delight to Betjeman is also a source of pain. Physical love is the occasion of guilt and remorse as much as it is of pleasure. The beauty of landscapes and buildings are constantly threatened by the speculator and the despoiler. Aware as he is of the joy of life, he is even more aware of its transitoriness. Death was the subject of his first printed poem and it has been the subject of most of his best poems since then; death and its attendant themes: guilt, doubt and loss.

The themes which have dominated Betjeman's verse are, in fact, indicated in the subjects of his three anthologies – *English, Scottish and Welsh Landscape* (1944), *English Love Poems* (1957) and *Altar and Pew* (1959). They are: places, love and religion. The sensitivity to place is apparent in all his work and is signalled in the number of poems which have place names as their title. It would be wrong, however, to think of him simply as a writer of descriptive topographical verses such as those turned out by the minor landscape poets whose work he loves so much. Many of the later pieces – 'Norfolk', 'Tregardock', 'Matlock Bath' – spring from the poet's sense of personal anguish rather than from his desire to capture in verse the impression of a particular place at a particular time. While in earlier poems such as 'Henley-on-Thames' Betjeman is only present as a tone of voice, in the later poems he is the subject, suffering, anxious and guilt-ridden. It is his gradual emergence from behind the veil of evasive irony which made possible the fine poems in *A Few Late Chrysanthemums*. Though apparently so homogeneous, his poetry has shown signs of that development which, since Yeats, poets have been expected to demonstrate. Physical love, another recurring theme, often treated farcically as in those poems which celebrate the Amazonian tigresses of suburban tennis courts, later became the subject of some of his saddest –

'Pershore Station, *or* A Liverish Journey First Class' – and some of his most macabre – 'Late Flowering Lust'. If one adds to these poems those which detail childhood humiliations, it sometimes seems that Betjeman has told us more about his own inner feelings than any other modern poet. This confessional posture does not invariably produce good poems though the absence of constraint, the compulsion to set down his deepest feelings, directly and candidly, was responsible for the change which occurred in his work during the mid forties.

The fun he had with 'High' and 'Low' and 'Broad' in the earlier poems gave way, in the later poems, to an honest examination of his own troubled Christian conscience, the agonies of doubt bordering on despair as well as a mature expression of his deep love for the Church of England: the hope it offers, the promise of eternal peace contained in the sacraments. Doubt has been responsible for some of his best poems. As he explained to Kenneth Allsop: 'Basically, I suppose I am not really a happy or cheerful man. It is an effort of will for me to believe that good will triumph . . . My only sustaining belief is that the Christian's faith is probably true. Why, then, should I fear death? Well, if you don't have doubts what would faith be? Doubts are the test of one's faith.' (*Lord I believe; help thou mine unbelief.*) He writes about death more honestly than any modern poet, with a sort of Victorian directness which only occasionally topples over into self-pity. In the very latest poems – 'Fruit' and 'Loneliness' – the avowed terror of some of the earlier poems has been succeeded by a sort of composure, proving that Betjeman has developed in this as in other ways.

Love, belief, death: these are hardly small themes. The still popular view that Betjeman has discovered a sort of poetry in dim suburbs, gaslit railway stations, and obscure watering-places and that his real achievement lies in this discovery, is very wide of the mark. Certainly such private interests cross-cut his poems, but they are the furnishing of the poems rather than their subject. The electrolier and the sepia-tinted views of Pinner in the station waiting-room are not the subject of 'The Metropolitan Railway'. The poem is about death and the loss of hope – 'Cancer has killed him. Heart is killing her.' The Edwardian bric-à-brac is expressive of the tragedy which is at the heart of the poem and not extraneous to it. Betjeman writes about what is human and, as we live our lives in the material world, this interest embraces the places, the buildings we inhabit, the clothes we wear, the railway stations we use, the cars we drive which, somehow, become expressive of us. Objects have a spiritual dimension for Betjeman: hence the 'wanton particularity' of his references to branded goods. This feature of his work has been effectively parodied by Alan Bennett in his brilliant piece, 'Place-Names of China', and might be called, *pace* Mr Amis, 'the Betjeman effect'. It is, of course, not the thing itself but its connection with human use which moves Betjeman. Nor is it a vague, nostalgic feeling for the associative qualities of places and objects. A precise, sharp concern for what is genuinely human animates all Betjeman's poems.

The achievement which Betjeman is most often credited with, by those who are not actively hostile to his work, is the presentation of the workings of a modern sensibility through traditional verse forms. This recalls Hardy's pronouncement that: 'All we can do is to write on the old themes in the old styles, but try to do a little better than those who went before us.' It is a definition of poetry which Betjeman would find acceptable. Like Hardy, Betjeman uses essentially Victorian forms to express the state of feeling of a suffering, sceptical, twentieth-century man. Almost all Betjeman's poems adopt traditional metres and, in many cases, these are direct cribs from other poets; he is by no means as metrically inventive as Hardy. This emerges very clearly in the characteristically self-deprecating description of the genesis of a poem which he wrote for the *Spectator*:

First there is the thrilling or terrifying recollection of a place, a person or a mood which hammers in the head saying, 'Go on! Go on! It is your duty to make a poem out of it.' Then a line or a phrase suggests itself. Next comes the selection of a metre. I am a traditionalist in metres and have made few experiments. The rhythms of Tennyson, Crabbe, Hawker, Dowson, Hardy, James Elroy Flecker, Moore and *Hymns A. and M.* are generally buzzing about in my brain and I choose one which seems to suit my theme. On the backs of cigarette packets and old letters, I write down my lines, crossing out and changing. When I return home I transfer the whole to foolscap and cross out and change again. Then I start reciting the lines aloud, either driving a car or on solitary walks until the sound of the verse satisfies me. Then I try reading the poem out to a patient friend whose criticisms I gladly accept provided they are of detail only. After that I may have the courage to send it all to a magazine.

There is something almost arbitrary in this selection of a suitable metre from a random stock always at the poet's disposal; it sounds rather like pulling down a bale of cloth to make a suite. One wonders, in fact, if the process is quite as conscious as he makes it seem; or if, more often than not, the poem chooses its own metre. By no means all the poems contain rhythmical and metrical echoes of other poets. If 'Devonshire Street' or 'I. M. Walter Ramsden' have precursors, I am unaware of them. Where the echoes are obvious, they are never intrusive or suggestive of parody; except where – as in 'Hymn' or 'Harvest Hymn' – Betjeman wants them to be in order to make a particular point or show a particular contrast. In his best poems, metre, subject and mood fuse perfectly, creating a satisfying poetic whole which is not dependent on awareness of the debt to another poet for its effect. None of these poems could be dismissed as derivative or slavishly imitative because the sensibility of the poet remains completely original. Betjeman has a unique tone of voice – hence the ease with which he can be parodied himself – and his poems are authentic and entirely personal in a way which the poems of C. Day Lewis, who had a similar ability to absorb influences, were not. When one reads 'Middlesex', one is aware of the Tennysonian echoes but one recognizes that only Betjeman could have written the poem. When one reads Day Lewis's 'The Unwanted', one is forced to conclude that Hardy could have done it better.

One of the reasons why Betjeman is 'a traditionalist in metres' is that he believes verse should have an auditory appeal. From the first, he wrote poems which yielded most of themselves when they were recited. The models he has chosen have tended to be those poets in whom musicality is pre-eminent: Dowson, Flecker, Tennyson. In this respect, he is a long way from contemporary poets who are inclined to disparage the sensual attraction of metre and rhyme; considering it dishonest, the sugar-coating of flatulent emotion and lack of intellectual rigour, rather as Ruskin thought stucco was a 'dishonest' material for architects to use. Although Betjeman's chief attraction for a certain type of reader is that he sticks to traditional forms, there is nothing cosy or reassuring in what the poems have to say. Of Betjeman it might truly be said his

'sweetest songs are those that tell of saddest thought'. In Clive
James's words: 'He can be called light-minded only by the thick-
witted, and this remains true even though the well-placed find him
comforting.'

It is unlikely that even Betjeman's most fervent admirers would
claim that he was a major poet. His best work has both depth and
sensitivity but one does not detect a powerful imagination – still less
a powerful intellect – at work in any of his poems. He is the poet of
the known world: illuminating odd corners, presenting human
emotion honestly and directly, and, thereby, enlarging the common
stock of available experience. Nowhere does he attempt to penetrate
beyond observable reality – even his religion is a very unmystical
and orthodox affair – and present Man in relation to the huge
abstracts: Time, Eternity, Nature. It would, of course, be unfair to
blame a poet for not doing what he never attempted or even claimed
to be able to do. Like Jane Austen, Betjeman has stuck to his little
piece of ivory. Social observation has been the basis of his art, as
it has with so many English poets, serious and unserious. Only
the visionaries – Blake, Lawrence, Hughes – are independent, indifferent to society and the absorbing subject of contemporary life
and manners. They, alone, are the re-makers, the exuberant ones
who get little or nothing for their poetry from their existence
in the 'civilized' everyday world of money, political parties, class-
distinction and organized religion.

Betjeman's very ordinariness, his common use of the common
language to express common experience is what endears him to
Philip Larkin. Larkin is very suspicious of the tendency towards
obscurity which characterizes a certain type of modern verse. This
is not mere obscurantism on his part; rather an awareness that
fraudulent talents find it easier to shelter behind huge and grandiose
abstractions, to pretend that these are the real stuff of poetry than
to present life as it is experienced by most people most of the time.
What Ted Hughes or Dylan Thomas, for instance, have said about
poetry could be made to sound like the utterances of charlatans,
egocentric mythmakers who have elevated the creative processes
above the humdrum business of earning a living and drawing
successive breaths, suggesting that the poet is a god-like visionary
set apart from his fellow men, like the Celtic saints in their bogs,
and gifted with unique and quasi-divine insight. Both Thomas and
Hughes are fine poets, of course. A problem arises only when every

poet claims to be their kind of poet and when critics assume that theirs is the only kind of poetry which it is permissible to write. Some of the hostility to Betjeman – if one ignores the academic priggishness which disdains anything which is popular – is grounded in this sort of assumption.

Betjeman's reputation, such as it is, is founded on what is really a very small output of poems. Auden believed that this was the sign of a minor poet, perhaps because he wrote so much himself. Unprolific poets are generally credited with perfectionism, inability to allow anything which does not show them at their best to be published; or they are accused of excessive caution or of having too limited a range. Most of these things have been said about Housman, for instance; only the last charge has been levelled against Betjeman. There are a number of bad or false poems in Housman and his range is far more limited then Betjeman's, though Betjeman never attains the emotional resonance and lyrical perfection of Housman at his best. The same might be said if one compares Betjeman with Larkin, who is about as unprolific as it is possible to be without abandoning writing altogether. ('Well, I speak to you as someone who hasn't written a poem for eighteen months.') Larkin's poems have a solid intellectual substructure, a technical complexity as well as an emotional authority which is beyond Betjeman: compare 'A Lincolnshire Church' with 'Church Going'. Larkin, however, though he writes about loss, failure, death and, in the process, affirms a kind of dogged strength, is not capable of those spontaneous celebrations of life which are an essential part of Betjeman's work. Larkin's 'Trees' only *seem* to say, 'Begin afresh, afresh, afresh' whereas Betjeman is lost for words as he beholds the 'reckless bestowing' of the natural world in 'Wantage Bells'. The difference between the two poets has been well expressed by Clive James: 'What is elegiac in Betjeman becomes tragic in Larkin. Betjeman is losing something he enjoyed, Larkin is losing what he never really had.'

Although much of the pleasure which Betjeman's verse gives is of the 'minimal' kind which Eliot detected in the best eighteenth-century verse, he is a poet whose response to experience, both visual and emotional, is direct and spontaneous. He says what he feels without self-consciousness. He is frightened of death and says so; he feels guilty about neglecting his parents and says so; he does not want his son to die and says so. His poems express his feelings directly, in the heat of the moment almost. He moves our hearts by showing his own. Though his directness does not always produce good poems, it is this impulse to set forward a moment and the emotion which it contains and to let it speak for itself which marks out such undeniably good poems as 'Devonshire Street' and 'In a Bath Teashop'. Although he runs the risk of sentimentality and self-pity in accepting the emotions of the moment as valid, Betjeman only rarely falls into these traps. In earlier poems he avoids them by the use of irony and subtle self-mockery, placing himself at an oblique angle to the poem. In later poems, they are avoided not by a device but simply by the patent sincerity of what he is saying and the genuine passion with which he says it. As Christopher Ricks said of the novels of Brian Moore, the strength of Betjeman's verse lies 'in their abolishing brow-distinction . . . by concentrating simply, directly, bravely on the primary sufferings and passions everybody feels'.

Certainly, he has altered our perception of the world around us. In lush Edwardian suburbs, in the little streets near provincial churches, in chapels-of-ease and in richly decorated Gothic Revival churches smoky with incense, what we see has been conditioned by our reading of Betjeman. To have enlarged experience in this way, to have mapped out a genuine country of the mind is, of course, no small achievement. But Betjeman is more than a topographer, more, even, than an emotional topographer; more than a curious searcher out of the obscure and the neglected; more than a connoisseur of the moment when a thing ceases to be characteristic and becomes suddenly charged with meaning; though he is all these things as well. He is not just a poetic eccentric, indulging minor interests, deftly manipulating traditional metres, piquantly turning his back on the technical experiment and innovation, the polymathic allusiveness, the elevation of difficulty which is characteristic of so much twentieth-century verse. He presents the human scene in its totality: the sadness of loss, failure and death, the joy of love, the delight of the visible world. His range is far from limited. In fact, he is limited only by what is human and, perhaps, by what is specifically English or, at least, British. He is certainly less circumscribed by narrow class attitudes than is often supposed, as the poem about the death of a lower-middle-class housewife and the savage piece about the upper-class Porkers show. His heroes are those innocent children of nature, the Pooters. He hates the masses only in the abstract. The individual souls which compose them inspire affection, even love, for they all have importance in God's eyes. It is this Christian sense of the importance of life which makes him more than a social reporter and more than a satirist. Although human beings are social animals, they are also God's creatures. He hates the levelling tendencies of mass democracy; the battery-house existence of modern industrial society; the package-deal opinions of an age of mass communication, not just because they threaten the aristocratic way of life to which he aspires but because they destroy individuality and so devalue mankind. Although many of his own values seem regressive or merely nostalgic, an honest reader would be hard pressed to deny the passion which underpins them. That so many have read and enjoyed his work is proof that these perceptions are not shared only by those of his age and class. Popularity may not be an infallible index of merit but nor is it to be used as evidence of its opposite. Dr Johnson's opinion of Gray's *Elegy* is apposite: 'I rejoice to concur with the common reader; for by the common sense of readers uncorrupted with literary prejudices, after all the refinements of subtilty and the dogmatism of learning, must be finally decided all claim to poetical honours.'

When they first began to appear, Betjeman's poems could have been likened to a little Gothick pavilion set in the landscape of modern verse; pretty and arresting in its way, but really just an ornamental fixture, oddly, if attractively, out of keeping with its surroundings. But, if the architectural allusion might be pushed further, this quaint little pavilion turned out, on closer examination, to look more like a church: a serious house on serious earth, which meant more to the people of the country than the grander buildings around it. And what could be heard inside were not the sounds of frivolous laughter; the indulgence of private jokes; the enactment of archaic rituals and facile sighs of *après nous le déluge*; but, rather, sincere and passionate statements about life and death which may yet prove more durable than some of the clever things being said behind other and more important-looking façades.

SELECT
BIBLIOGRAPHY

(All titles are published in London, unless otherwise stated.)

BOOKS BY BETJEMAN

Mount Zion, James Press, 1931 (facsimile reissue, St James Press, 1975).

Ghastly Good Taste, Chapman & Hall, 1933 (revised edition with a new autobiographical preface, Blond & Briggs, 1970).

Continual Dew, John Murray, 1937 (facsimile reissue, John Murray, 1977).

An Oxford University Chest, John Miles, 1938 (reissued in paperback by Oxford University Press, 1979).

Old Lights for New Chancels, John Murray, 1940.

Vintage London, Collins, 1942.

English Cities and Small Towns: Britain in Pictures, Collins, 1943.

John Piper: Penguin Modern Painters, Penguin, 1944.

New Bats in Old Belfries, John Murray, 1945.

Slick But Not Streamlined: poetry and prose selected and with an introduction by W. H. Auden, Doubleday, New York, 1947.

Selected Poems: selected with an introduction by John Sparrow, John Murray, 1948.

First and Last Loves, John Murray, 1952.

A Few Late Chrysanthemums, John Murray, 1954.

Poems in the Porch, S.P.C.K., 1954.

The English Town in the Last Hundred Years: The Rede Lecture, 1956, Cambridge University Press, 1956.

Collected Poems: compiled with an introduction by Lord Birkenhead, John

Murray, 1958 (1962 edition contains additional poems from the early collections; 1970 edition contains *High and Low*; and 1979 edition contains *A Nip in the Air*).

Collins Guide to English Parish Churches: edited with a long introduction by John Betjeman, Collins, 1958.

Summoned by Bells, John Murray, 1960.

High and Low, John Murray, 1966.

A Pictorial History of English Architecture, John Murray, 1972.

London's Historic Railway Stations, John Murray, 1972.

A Nip in the Air, John Murray, 1974.

Archie and the Strict Baptists, John Murray, 1977.

The Best of Betjeman: poetry and prose selected by John Guest, John Murray, 1978.

Church Poems, John Murray, 1981.

Uncollected Poems, John Murray, 1982.

GENERAL BOOKS

ALLSOP, KENNETH, *Scan*, Hodder & Stoughton, 1965.

BOWRA, C. M., *Memories: 1898–1939*, Weidenfeld & Nicolson, 1966.

BROOKE, JOCELYN, *Ronald Firbank and John Betjeman*: Writers and Their Work, Longmans for the British Council, 1966.

DAVIE, DONALD, *Thomas Hardy and British Poetry*, Routledge, 1973.

GREEN, R. L., and HOOPER, W., *C. S. Lewis*, Fount Paperbacks, 1979.

JAMES, CLIVE, *At the Pillars of Hercules*, Cape, 1979.

KERMODE, FRANK, *Puzzles and Epiphanies*, Routledge, 1962.

LANCASTER, OSBERT, *With an Eye to the Future*, John Murray, 1967.

MACNEICE, LOUIS, *The Strings Are False*, Faber, 1965.

PRESS, JOHN, *John Betjeman*: Writers and Their Work, Longmans for the British Council, 1974 (contains a useful bibliography).

RICHARDS, J. M., *Memoirs of an Unjust Fella*, Weidenfeld & Nicolson, 1980.

STANFORD, DEREK, *John Betjeman: A Study*, Neville Spearman, 1961.

STAPLETON, MARGARET L., *Sir John Betjeman: A Bibliography of Writings by and about Him*: The Scarecrow Author Bibliographies, No. 21, Scarecrow Press, New Jersey, 1974.

WAIN, JOHN, *Essays on Literature and Ideas*, Macmillan, 1963.

WAUGH, EVELYN, *Diaries*: edited by Michael Davie, Weidenfeld & Nicolson, 1976; *Letters*: edited by Mark Amory, Weidenfeld & Nicolson, 1980.

ARTICLES

BARNES, SUSAN, 'Betjeman, I Bet Your Racket Brings You In a Pretty Packet', *Sunday Times Magazine*, 30 January 1972.

BERGONZI, BERNARD, 'Culture and Mr Betjeman', *Twentieth Century*, February 1965.

CROOKSTON, PETER, 'Reflections on the Poet at Three Score Years and Ten', *Observer*, 22 August 1976.

DAVIE, MICHAEL, 'The Bard of the Railway Gas-lamp', *Observer*, 15 October 1972.

DRIBERG, TOM, 'A Walk with Mr Betjeman', *New Statesman*, 6 January 1961.

LARKIN, PHILIP, 'Betjeman En Bloc', *Listen*, Spring 1959; 'The Blending of Betjeman', *Spectator*, 2 December 1960; 'It Could Only Happen in England', *Cornhill Magazine*, Autumn 1971.

PRESS, JOHN, 'Ever-later Chrysanthemums', *The Times Literary Supplement*, 10 January 1975.

RECORDS BY BETJEMAN

The World of Sir John Betjeman, Argo PA 339.

Summoned by Bells: Selections Read by John Betjeman, Argo PLP 1069.

Betjeman's Banana Blush: music by Jim Parker, Charisma CAS 1086.

Sir John Betjeman's Britain: music by Jim Parker, Charisma CAS 1130.

Late Flowering Love: music by Jim Parker, Charisma CAS 1096.

Sir John Betjeman's 'Varsity Rag: music by Jim Parker, Charisma CAS 1154.